Natural
Learning
and
Mathematics

Natural Learning and Mathematics

*Rex Stoessiger
and
Joy Edmunds*

With a Foreword by Hilary Shuard

Heinemann
Portsmouth, NH

Thomas Nelson
Melbourne, Australia

Heinemann Educational Books, Inc.
361 Hanover Street   Portsmouth, NH 03801-3959
Offices and agents throughout the world

Published simultaneously in Australia by
Thomas Nelson Australia
102 Dodds Street   South Melbourne 3205

Library of Congress Cataloging-in-Publication Data
Stoessiger, Rex.
   Natural learning and mathematics / Rex Stoessiger and Joy Edmunds ; with a foreword by Hilary Shuard.
      p.   cm.
   Includes bibliographical references.
   ISBN 0-435-08328-7
   1. Mathematics—Study and teaching (Primary)   I. Edmunds, Joy. II. Title.
QA135.5.S757   1992
372.7'044—dc20   *91-46271*
                                                        CIP

National Library of Australia Cataloguing in Publication Data
Stoessiger, Rex.
   Natural learning and mathematics.
   Bibliography.
   ISBN 0 17 008825 1.
   1. Mathematics—Study and teaching (Primary).   2. Language experience approach in education.   I. Edmunds, Joy.   II. Title.
372.7044

Designed by Maria Szmauz
Cover drawings by Grade 2/3, Waimea Heights Primary School
Photos by Geoff Tyson
Printed in the United States of America
92 93 94 95 96 10 9 8 7 6 5 4 3 2 1

Contents

Foreword
Hilary Shuard

Very young children learn to talk from the people around them, by a method that can be described as a "natural learning process." Some teachers introduce and extend similar natural learning processes at school, when children are developing their learning of language; these approaches to language teaching are often very successful.

This book applies the idea of "natural learning processes" to the teaching of mathematics in primary schools. The authors have developed their ideas while working with groups of teachers in Tasmania over a period of several years; the book is firmly based on the practical classroom experience of the authors and of the teachers with whom they work. Suggestions are made about ways in which children can be challenged to explore mathematics in their own ways, to refine their thinking, to explain it orally and in writing, and to publish the best of their mathematical writing for their classmates to read and build upon.

The authors urge that the study of most facets of mathematics, throughout the primary years and beyond, should be approached through a variety of open-ended mathematical "challenges" that children can tackle in their own ways. Children's work on these challenges always draws upon their own personal mathematical understanding and knowledge; some challenges can also allow children to explore mathematical ideas that are new to them.

The fact that children are encouraged to express their mathematics in a personal way also gives the teacher insight into which mathematical ideas a child should work on next. Children's mistakes in reasoning or calculation can be regarded as "first approximations" that the child can improve upon, rather than as crimes that ruin the correctness of the work. When they work in this way; children lose any fear of failure, since they can respond to the challenges at their own level.

Many primary teachers are looking for ways of teaching mathematics that involve the children more vigorously in their own learning. This book has much to offer to those teachers. The teachers who worked with these authors found that the teaching of mathematics also became a more interesting and enjoyable activity for themselves. Any teacher who responds to the challenges set in this book will undoubtedly find an increasing level of personal enjoyment and interest in mathematics teaching.

Acknowledgments

M ost of the ideas presented in this book were developed in conjunction with classroom teachers. There are too many to thank individually, but we very much wish to acknowledge our debt to their enthusiasm and professionalism that made developing a new approach to mathematics education possible.

We thank the following teachers and their students who directly contributed material for the book: Anne Barwick, Corrine Dorsett, Pam Eaves, Andrea Gatward, Dale James, Pat Jeffery, Pamela Longridge, Kathie McKeown, Petrie Murchison, Doug Miller, Jan Thompson, Lyn Thompson, Amanda Vautin, and Jenny Williams. Special thanks to Andrea Gatward, Pat Jeffrey, Kathie McKeown, and Doug Miller (and their students) for allowing us to photograph in their classrooms.

We acknowledge the considerable editorial assistance of Michael Ginsberg in developing an acceptable manuscript and the continuing support of Toby Gordon of Heinemann in initiating the project and seeing it through many difficulties.

We also acknowledge the support of our employer, The Tasmanian Department of Education and the Arts. The views expressed, however, are solely those of the authors.

Natural
Learning
and
Mathematics

Chapter One

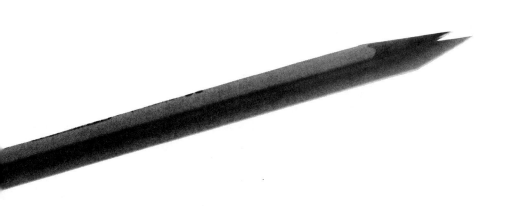

Natural Learning and Mathematics

*L*ook inside an elementary classroom where natural language-learning processes are respected and celebrated. Children's writing is displayed all around the walls and hangs from the ceiling as well. Printed material is everywhere. Big books, posters, lists, and teacher-made displays are beautifully presented, designed to catch the eye, geared toward making literature exciting. Much of the children's writing is typed (often by parent helpers) and then illustrated by the young authors.

Children are discussing their reading and writing. Some are talking with friends, some with older students, and some with the teacher. There's an active buzz of conversation as the children work.

Looking more closely, we see refinement processes in operation. Children are working on their first drafts, editing their drafts, using resources in the classroom to check their spelling, and preparing a final version for publication.

We hear teachers and students discussing the quality of the work produced. Does this say what you wished it to? Is the ending what you wanted? Is it long enough to communicate what you are trying to say? Too long? Is it good enough to publish?

We see students who clearly enjoy what they are doing. In fact, they are eager to tell us about it. They show us—with pride—their published work and talk of themselves as authors.

Then return a little later, when math class is in progress.

Look around for the evidence of math work. There's a collection of equilateral triangles on the bulletin board, but nothing else. However, students are "doing" mathematics. Some solitary workers are struggling away at a list of sums. Physical prop-type aids are readily available.

The action goes something like this: $6 + 4 = ?$ First count out one, two, three, four, five, six blocks. Now count out four more. One, two, three, four. Now put them together and count the group. One, two . . . ten. Next write the number 10 in your book and move quickly to the next question: $7 +$

4 = ? Count out seven blocks, and so on. The students' finished work looks like this:

(a) 10
(b) 11
(c) 6

With the exercises finished, the work is collected by the teacher.

Now the students move on to time problems. Everyone takes out a clock stamp. "Stamp the clock face on your book ten times," the teacher says. "Then mark the position of the hands for three o'clock, four o'clock . . . half past eight."

Or, students may be measuring: "With your ruler make a line that is four centimeters long." Or, "Use centicubes to find out how long the pen, the book, and the box are."

Had enough? We had. Driving from school to school in Tasmania, Australia—an enterprise that can take many hours—we had plenty of time to consider and discuss what we were seeing in language and mathematics classrooms. The conversation gradually worked its way to a deceptively simple idea. What if mathematics were taught in the same way as language? What would teachers do? What would students do? What would we see in classrooms? Wouldn't it be more enjoyable? Wouldn't students learn more than they seemed to glean from the diet of sums and exercises we were seeing?

The simple idea that mathematics teaching and learning could be more like teaching and learning language was enough to get us started on a curriculum development project in Tasmania. It gave us, and the teachers we worked with, an initial aim and a readily accessible model that could be drawn from to suggest beginning approaches and to answer questions when the path was not so obvious.

We were very quickly forced to clarify our ideas, including what we meant by using a language approach to teach mathematics. Teachers who had heard about this approach from others were interpreting using language techniques for mathematics quite literally: Some began to use big books with numbers scattered through the stories, while others emphasized mathematical story problems to the exclusion of other work. While we have no particular objection to mathematical big books or story problems, we came to recognize these adaptations of language techniques as too literal. We realized our aim was to transfer the processes and conditions underlying language learning, not to copy the techniques.

The language approach should be seen as an analogy, a metaphor, in the development of a new method of teaching mathematics. When we ask a teacher, as we often do, "What would you do if this were a language situation?" we are hoping to focus on the underlying strategies and are seeking to find ways in which these strategies can be adapted to mathematics. If the teacher answers, "Well, I would ask [the student] to edit her draft so it is ready for publication," we don't then suggest that students check the spelling in their mathematics work. Instead, we look for mathematical analogies to editing. How do mathematicians refine their work? They certainly check to make sure it is mathematically correct. Students also need to check their work to ensure that the arithmetic is correct and that the mathematical meaning is clear before the work is displayed.

We do want students to use more language to support their mathematics learning. It is through open discussion that mathematical understanding is developed, concepts are formed, and the appropriate mathematical vocabulary and language structures are practiced and modeled. It is through language that students make meaning of their mathematical experiences and develop confidence in what they have learned.

Most important, we desire the new approach to be essentially mathematical. It must suit the ideas and methods of mathematics. Just as we model the writing process on the activities of adult writers, so also we must find out what real mathematics users actually do and use that as our classroom model.

Finally, we want students to learn to think mathematically. We want them not only to have mathematical skills but to be able to apply their skills in thoughtful ways to new situations. We want students who use mathematics capably in the world and who learn for themselves by applying their mathematical theories in practical situations. And we want students to enjoy both mathematics and learning. In language class, teachers aim to create students who can read, who do read, who learn by reading, and who enjoy reading. We see no reason to accept anything less for mathematics. We also insist that the capacities of thinking mathematically, of using, learning, and enjoying mathematics, be developed simultaneously. We are not willing to sacrifice one for the others.

To know what we want from mathematics education is one thing. To be able to deliver it is quite another. Our simple idea that mathematics could be taught in ways analogous to language needed to be turned into a practical classroom program if it was to be useful to teachers. To do this, we recruited teachers willing to try out the new approach in their classrooms. Initially, we enlisted those known to be successful teachers of language. We reasoned that teachers who were applying the language ideas successfully would be in the best position to attempt to adapt these ideas to mathematics.

In working with teachers, we alternated theory with practice, workshops with classroom trials. Initially, we asked the teachers to consider how they might adapt language-learning conditions for mathematics. The key question, again, was: "If this were a language situation what would you do?" The ideas developed in the workshops were tried out by teachers during the three- or four-week gap between workshops. They were asked to monitor what happened and to bring examples of student work to share at the next workshop.

Each subsequent workshop began with a sharing session. As a result, teachers reflected on their developing practice and came up with new ideas to try in the classroom. When possible, we visited teachers in their classrooms, so we could sit down with some students working at a mathematics activity. This proved valuable both in providing support for teachers and in keeping our own feet firmly on the classroom floor.

The reactions of teachers trying out the new approach convinced us that something worthwhile was being developed. Time and again, we abandoned our planned agendas for the workshops and let the teachers take over with descriptions of the exciting changes that were happening in their classrooms.

Our initial group consisted of just ten teachers who investigated the new approach for a term. Their success encouraged us to expand the workshop program, running it for an entire year and making it widely available to interested teachers.

This book is being written less than four years after the formulation of our initial idea. In that time, this idea has become a full-fledged theory of teaching and learning with a strong base of classroom practice to support it. In many primary schools in this (small) state, at least one teacher has been exposed to these methods; in several schools, the entire staff is working in the new way. A number of secondary school teachers have also become interested and are trying these methods with their students.

Our role has been first to initiate this work, then to support teachers as they try out the new approach, and finally to collect examples from classroom situations that reveal something of what happens when a natural learning approach is adopted.

We'd like to introduce the notion of natural learning approaches to mathematics by sharing a few vignettes from our classroom observances. From there, we move on to the theory underpinning natural learning processes. Then, we examine classroom challenges in detail, as a means of creating a natural learning environment. Finally, we look at classroom structure, curriculum, and assessment.

As you read the following vignettes, remember the earlier descriptions of the classroom in which language learning was taking place and the one in which mathematics was being taught through a traditional approach. Also, notice that the engagements are framed as "challenges" by the teachers. The notion of challenges is crucial to our framework for teaching mathematics. We will discuss them in detail in Chapter 4. For now, sit back and listen to the language of mathematics.

Measuring the ball

In a classroom of six- and seven-year-olds, the teacher begins the lesson with some mental arithmetic. The children sit on the mat around her and she records their responses on an easel. "Today's number is 13," she says. "What equations can you make for 13?" As the children volunteer answers, she records them on the easel: $10 + 3 = 13$, $12 + 1 = 13$, and so on. When a multiplication example is volunteered, the teacher records that in a separate column; she does the same with subtractions.

The teacher frequently asks how the student performed the calculation and then asks if other students have used a different method. Usually they have. As a result, the class is exposed to a variety of ways to perform particular calculations. If there is disagreement about an answer, the emphasis is on the reasoning used, not just on getting a correct answer.

After about ten minutes of mental arithmetic, the teacher shows the class a soccer ball and challenges her students to think of the different things about the ball they could measure. (Since this is the first time the teacher is proposing a measurement challenge, she deliberately chooses a broad challenge to give her an indication of their capabilities.)

The class discusses the challenge and several suggestions are made. These include measuring the length around the outside (circumference), weighing the ball, and measuring some of the shapes (pentagons) on the ball.

The teacher explains that because there is only one ball and lots of students, she would like each of them to find an opportunity to work on the challenge when the ball is free. The students then continue their existing work while one student starts measuring the ball.

Over the next few weeks, individual students try different approaches to measurement. James writes the letters of his name in a line around the ball and determines that it is 52 letters long—ten times his name and two more letters. Anthony traces his hand and measures the length to the tip of his middle finger with a ruler. It's 17 centimeters. He then places his hand on the ball and marks successive hand lengths, determining that his hand fits around it four times with a little left over. He measures the remaining bit with a ruler and records the total length as "4 hands + 5cm."

Anthony's teacher challenges him further, asking him how he could translate his answer into centimeters. Anthony collects the Unifix™ cubes and draws out four lots, each consisting of 17 blocks. He reorders his collection of blocks into groups of ten, counts the eight left over and records 68. He puts away the Unifix™ blocks and realizes he now has to calculate 68 + 5. He walks over to the "1 to 100" chart on the wall, finds 68 and moves forward five more numbers, much to the delight of his teacher.

While Anthony is counting the blocks, his friend, Nick, who is watching, says, "It's 68." His teacher asks how he worked it out and he explains, "I know two 15s are 30, and then I need four more for the 17s, that makes 34. So another 30 makes 64 and four more is 68."

On another occasion, Rose asks the teacher if she can fill

the empty aquarium. She returns later to ask if it is okay to put textacolor marks on the side. Intrigued, the teacher follows Rose to the tank to investigate. Rose had initially poured water in the tank and is now attempting to submerge the ball to find its volume. She adds more water, enough to submerge the ball. She then finds she has to wait for the water to settle, first to mark the height of the water without the ball and then to mark the height with the ball submerged. After a considerable effort, she has two marks placed to her satisfaction. She then measures the change in water height with a ruler and records the result as three centimeters.

The teacher explains, "It was more than enough that Rose had the idea of measuring the volume of the ball by immersing it in water and that she found a way to do so. It took a long time and it would have been inappropriate for me to have challenged her to further refine her volume measurement on this occasion. It was just great to see her thinking about measurements developing in this way."

Rose records her initial results on a sheet of paper, which is damp and crumpled by the time she is finished. Later, she prepares a report of her work, complete with diagrams, which is then published for display in the classroom.

Rose is taking responsibility for her own learning, just as James and Anthony have done. She has also taken advantage of a classroom that is rich in invitations and tools for learning, as have James and Anthony. Rose has determined which aspect of measuring she will attend to and has developed her own method for making the measurement. Her teacher accepts it as an approximation of adult ways of measuring volume, just as she has accepted James's and Anthony's work.

A big book in math

In a classroom of ten- to twelve-year-olds, we notice first the published mathematics. Along with the language work, the math artifacts cover all the available wall space and hang from strings extended across the ceiling. Mathematics books, made by students, fill the bookcases, alongside big books on mathematical themes containing contributions from the whole class. Students are immersed in mathematics, most of it of their own making.

In this classroom, the teacher begins the lesson by discussing the new curtains she plans to buy for her living room windows. She provides the dimensions and the class determines how much material would be needed to cover the windows, including estimates of the extra needed at the edges and for hems, and then discusses the pleating of curtains and how that might affect the amount of material required. The teacher indicates later that she had planned to introduce some work on measurement in a few weeks and that she wanted to provide early demonstrations of measuring and its usefulness.

After about twenty minutes, the teacher closes the discussion on curtains and reminds the class that they had earlier been examining some sales catalogues and the various discounts offered on different items. She then challenges them to make their own sales catalogue and to indicate the discounts offered and the prices.

As the students work on this challenge, the teacher records her observations of the different methods they use for calculating discounts. Later, she will record the different methods used by the students, along with a few of her own, in a big book. This becomes a class resource for calculating discounts. Here are excerpts from the book, *Our Class Book of Discounts*:

When I used to go shopping with my dad he used a quick method in his head. I'll try that next. I have

children's trousers costing $12.00 and shoes costing $70.00. I want to have 10% discount off both prices. Dad used to move the decimal point one place to the left. So for the trousers:

Normal price—$12.00

To find 10% of the price, $12.00 becomes $1.20. (We drop off the final zero because there are 2 numerals after the decimal point with money.)

Discount off the normal price:
$$
\begin{array}{r}
\$12.00 \\
- \ \$1.20 \\
\hline
\$10.80
\end{array}
$$

The new price is $10.80.

Looking at this method reminds me of what I saw Adam doing when he was finding 40% of some prices.

I'll try his method next. I have a little girl's dress
costing $20.00 and I want 40% discount off the price.
Adam's method went like this:
Normal price—$20.00
10% of price—$20.00 becomes $2.00
40% is 4 × 10%
And 4 × $2.00 = $8.00
Discount off the normal price: $20.00
                                   − $8.00
                                     $12.00

New price—$12.00.

Discovering rules

Kelly, age eleven, attempts a challenge proposed by the
teacher:

> Some people say that, to add four consecutive
> numbers, you add the first and last numbers and
> multiply by two. What can you find out about this?

Kelly quickly satisfies herself that the rule seems to work for
four numbers; she then starts investigating its application to
larger groups. In all she comes up with three rules. Her first
rule (Figure 1–1) is clearly an extension of the result for four
numbers. As one can see, Kelly has extended the idea of
consecutive numbers to "consecutive fractions" and finds
that her rule also seems to work for these.

Kelly's second rule, for ten consecutive numbers, is even
more complicated than the first but by the third rule (Figure
1–2) Kelly has developed a more elegant theory. Kelly's
teacher ensures that all three rules are published in the classroom so that they can be used by other children, to learn
from, to test, and to use as the basis for further work.

My Theory :-

If you want to add 6 consecutive numbers add the first and last number together & multiply by 2. Then add the two middle numbers and add to your previous answer

E.G. $1+2+3+4+5+6=21$

$$(1+6)\times 2 + (3+4)$$
$$7$$
$$14+7=21$$

$$\frac{1}{6}+\frac{2}{6}+\frac{3}{6}+\frac{4}{6}+\frac{5}{6}+\frac{6}{6}=\frac{21}{6}=3\frac{3}{6} \text{ or } 3\frac{1}{2}$$

$$\left(\frac{1}{6}+\frac{6}{6}\right)\times 2 + \left(\frac{3}{6}+\frac{4}{6}\right)$$

$$\left(\frac{7}{6}\times\frac{2}{1}\right)+\frac{7}{6}$$

$$\frac{14}{6}+\frac{7}{6}=\frac{21}{6}=3\frac{3}{6} \text{ or } 3\frac{1}{2}$$

Figure 1–1.   Kelly's rule for adding six consecutive numbers.

My Theory:-

If you want to add 20 consecutive

numbers you add the first and the last

and multiply by 10.

E.G. $1+2+3+4+5+6+7+8+9+10+11+12+13+14+15+16+17+18+19+20 = 210$

$(1+\overset{21}{20}) \times 10 = 210$

Figure 1-2. Kelly's rule for adding twenty consecutive numbers.

Kelly explains one of the rules she has discovered.

Meanwhile Darryl publishes the rule:

Darryl's Rule: For [adding] an even amount of consecutive numbers you add the first and last numbers and multiply by half the number of consecutive numbers.

15

Adam reads Darryl's rule and publishes:

1 + 2 + 3 + 4 + 5 + 6 + 7 + 8 + 9 + 10 + 11 +
12 + 13 + 14 + 15 + 16 + 17 + 18 +
19 + 20 + 21 + 22 + 23 + 24 + 25 + 26 = 351
1 + 26 = 27
27 × 13 = 351
1 + 2 + 3 + ... + 53 + 54 = 1485
54 + 1 = 55
55 × 27 = 1485
Darryl's Rule is correct.

The next challenge posed to these students was:

Investigate the ways of getting the average of
consecutive numbers. Can you come up with a
formula? Write a letter or newspaper report of your
findings.

Mathew soon notices that for an odd number of consecutive
numbers the average is the same as the middle number. He
wrote the following letter to Troy.

Dear Troy

I'm writing to tell you about a brilliant Challenge that
we are doing at school. It's great. Here's a couple of
examples.

21 + 22 + 23 + 24 + 25 + 26 + 27 = 168
168 ÷ 7 = 24

And my theory is, to find the average of an odd
number of consecutive numbers look at the middle
number. Then add up all your consecutive numbers
then divide by the number of consecutive numbers
you have. The answer will be the same as the middle
number.

I hope you try this method.

From
Mathew

PS Write back.

Meanwhile Jackie finds that the average of four consecutive numbers can be found by adding the first and last numbers and dividing by two. She then tries this out for other groups of consecutive numbers and decides that it is a general rule. She goes on to publish her results as a news story, shown in Figure 1–3.

Figure 1–3. Jackie's news story on the averages of consecutive numbers.

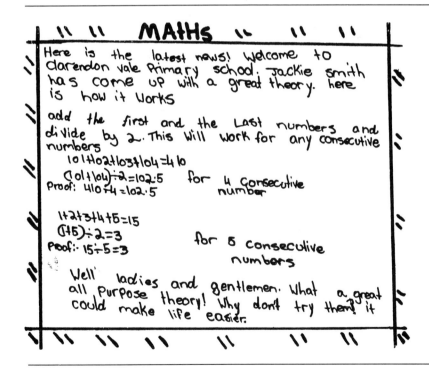

True for any number

What things are true for any number? For example,
anynumber + anynumber = 2 × anynumber. Record
your findings and select the most interesting to
publish.

We present this challenge to the class of eleven-and twelve-
year-olds and ask for suggestions. Several responses, similar
to the example, are forthcoming. We list them on the board,
using "anyno" as an abbreviation for anynumber. Where
two numbers are involved we write, for example, anyno +
otherno = otherno + anyno. We substitute a few numbers
for the "anyno" to reassure ourselves that the expressions
really do seem to be true for any number.

When the students have clarified the challenge, they are
asked to work in friendship groups of two or three to respond. A few find it difficult to start and need more individual discussion, but soon all are at work on an activity that
lasts more than an hour.

The first examples produced are fairly simple. Judy records: "Anyno times same anyno, divided by same anyno =
anyno."

Naomi first writes "78 + 48 − 78 = 48; 48 + 78 − 48
= 78" and then produces "Anyno divided by 2 = ½ itself,
and anyno − 1 + 1 = anyno, and anyno times 4 divided by
4 = anyno."

Clara records:

For this rule you require a multiple of 3 (M.O.3)
(M.O.3) divided by 2 divided by 3 × 6 = same
(M.O.3)
24 ÷ 2 ÷ 3 × 6 = 24
3 ÷ 2 (1.5) ÷ 3 (0.5) × 6 = 3

Angela first writes "3 × 3 = 9." She then writes "Anyno ×
anyno = a square number." She finally publishes the two
rules shown in Figure 1–4, using *A* to stand for any number.

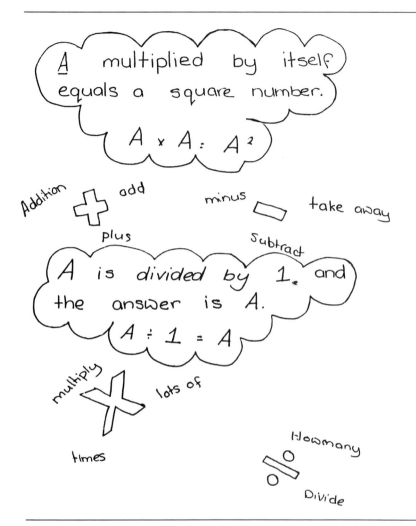

Figure 1—4.   Angela's true-for-any-number rules.

David writes, "Any number × 100% = any number," and provides examples.

Three girls working together discover and record a rule:

Any no. plus itself divided by ½ of itself = 4
e.g., 7 + 7 divided by 3.5 = 4

This is intriguingly simple, so we ask the girls to display their rule on the board for others to investigate further. Later in the session, the girls also produce:

Anyno. plus itself ÷ ¼ of itself = 8
e.g., (8 + 8) ÷ 2 = 8
Anyno. plus itself ÷ ⅓ of itself = 6
e.g., (3 + 3) ÷ 1 = 6

These rules became the bases for challenges in subsequent lessons as students tested and extended them.

While this work is in progress, we use the girls' first rule—any number plus itself divided by ½ itself = 4—to demonstrate algebra to the class. With language, we often surround learners with complicated words and expressions well before we expect the learners to use those words and expressions. Similarly, we feel students should be shown more complicated mathematics well before they are required to use it.

We explain that we are intrigued by the first rule, and wish to investigate why it seems to work. As we explore, we substitute a for "anyno." One student asks why we have done that, and we explain that any letter or symbol would do. We propose using the student's initial on the next occasion.

Most members of the class seem to follow what has been explained; others look somewhat bemused. However, since they are not required to do anything with this information in the immediate future, their understanding is not an issue.

More important, the students are seeing formal algebra being used for practical purposes well before they are required to deal with it themselves. The mystique—and anxiety—is gone. In a meaningful context, we are demonstrating mathematical ideas—ideas that are more advanced than the learners could fully deal with—just as parents do quite naturally with language.

We finish the session with a sharing time. All the students contribute what they consider their most interesting anynumber rule, and we list them on the board. This gives all students the chance to see the wide variety of expressions that have been generated and invites them to comment on one another's work.

A language-rich experience. In a math class.

Chapter Two

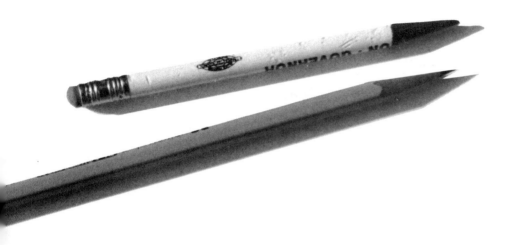

Natural Learning
Theory

A solid body of theory and research supports the view that children are natural learners. Young children learn an enormous amount of language and mathematics, quite naturally, before they come to school. They learn to talk. They learn much of the mathematical language of space (up, down, beside, above, next to) and of relationships (bigger, longer, taller, wider, heavier, slower). Many have working ideas about number ("I'm three and I'll be four next"), order (first, second, last), and even fractions ("I want the biggest half")! The conditions that operate to allow this learning to occur are called natural learning conditions. They describe what most parents do without even thinking about it to help their children learn. They are—whether consciously or not—what the teachers in the language and math classrooms described in Chapter 1 appear to have been striving for.

Natural learning conditions relative to language, in particular children's acquisition of their oral language capabilities, have been studied in detail. Learning to talk requires children to master thousands of arbitrary conventions with little intrinsic logic and with highly complex social and personal differences in usages.

It is a stunning achievement.

Learning to speak the language of the culture into which we are born is such a successful, easy, painless task, and it occurs with such monotonous regularity and success, that we take it for granted and overlook the enormity of the task (see Cambourne 1988, p. 30). Clearly, it is of value to teachers to understand the conditions that make this achievement possible with the hope that they might be used for other forms of language (and mathematical) learning.

Brian Cambourne (1988) has conceptualized these conditions under the following headings:

Immersion

Demonstration

Engagement

Expectation

Responsibility

Use

Approximation

Response

Cambourne notes that young children are immersed in a language-rich environment with innumerable demonstrations of language use in contexts that help indicate the meaning being conveyed. Children are highly engaged in using language, while adults have absolute expectations that their children will learn to talk. Yet the responsibility for this learning remains with the child. Children decide which aspects of language they will attend to, and they have many opportunities to use their emerging language ideas. Adults support their children by readily accepting even very rough approximations of adult language and by responding in meaningful ways.

Many teachers throughout the world have now developed ways to adapt the same conditions for the classroom to enhance mastery of language in reading and writing. When established in the classroom, these learning conditions allow natural learning processes to operate. The learning itself is quite idiosyncratic. It is regulated and paced by the learner and is always purposeful. It does not seem to have a predictable course or set stages, but it is developmental, in that learners move toward the common goal of becoming independent learners of language in all its forms.

At the same time as views on teaching and learning language have changed, so have ideas about mathematics and mathematics education. Mathematics is no longer seen as purely concerned with complex rules and symbols. It is more commonly viewed as a sign system, a tool for making sense of that part of the world dealing with quantity, size, and shape.

Since language has its beginnings in the struggle to make sense of the world and to convey meaning to others, it seems obvious that language has an important role in the learning of mathematics. Students require meaningful mathematical experiences with ample time for talking, both self-talk and shared talk. In this way, mathematical ideas are developed. Through exploratory talk, students use their own words to describe what they are doing, seeing, and thinking and to refine their theories. With encouragement, students will also experiment with the representation of their thinking on paper. Since writing and thinking are related, this experimentation allows the student to reflect on experiences and ideas and provides a means of communicating with others.

This connection between mathematics and language has led us to investigate how the conditions and processes that teachers provide to promote effective language learning can be adapted for mathematics. Teachers have found that some of these conditions and processes can be readily transferred to the mathematics area, while others are best used metaphorically as models for the mathematics classroom. The rest of this chapter outlines the above-mentioned conditions and how they might apply to mathematics.

Immersion

Young children are continually in contact with people purposefully using language in all its modes. From this, they quite naturally gain a wealth of data that enables them to develop a wide understanding of language use and structure. As Cambourne (1988) explains, "From the moment they are born young language learners are saturated in the medium they are expected to learn" (p. 32). Cambourne emphasizes that the language "is always whole, usually meaningful, and in a context which makes sense, or from which sense can be construed'' (p. 34).

Much of this language use is mathematical. Children are immersed in numerical and spatial language; they hear and see people measuring, positioning, counting, using money, telling time, and making and recognizing patterns and relationships. They naturally learn to use much of this language for themselves and become effective mathematical communicators.

We believe that it is similarly important that teachers continue to immerse students in a mathematics-rich environment in schools. Immersion is fostered when teachers use mathematics often, for real purposes and in a variety of ways. Teachers can display mathematics and ensure that students have access to a wide variety of materials and equipment. We live in a world that is replete with mathematics, but too often it is hidden from students. Teachers can make it more available by talking about the mathematical aspects of the

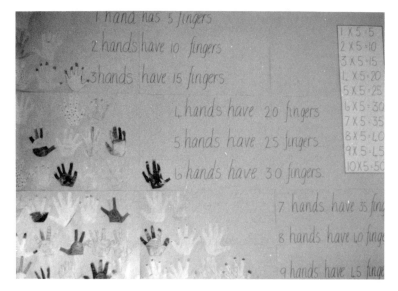

Immersion: The 5 times table in a kindergarten classroom.

Immersion in a mathematics-rich environment.

world or drawing the attention of students to the mathematics in their environment. Teachers of young children do not seem to have difficulty doing this. However, it becomes more difficult in classrooms of older students, possibly because the mathematics has become more abstract and less practical.

It is essential that the mathematics be in context and be meaningful if learners are to find it useful. If an architectural plan of the school and a survey map of the school grounds are displayed in the classroom, for example, there is enough contextual information available for interested students to extract some meaning from them, even if the students are not yet able to fully understand either.

One teacher of five- and six-year-olds decided to immerse her students in clocks and their use for telling time. She started the activity by challenging her students to design a clock for themselves. The students drew a variety of clock faces—several hard to recognize as such. Several of the children did not put numbers on their clocks. Others used numbers beyond 12, or squashed all the numbers together on the right side of the clock.

For the next two weeks, the teacher filled the school day with clocks. The students collected every clock they could and displayed them in the classroom. (Many were brought from home.) They read and wrote stories about clocks, shared rhymes and sang songs about clocks, and played with clocks. The teacher referred to the time displayed on the clocks whenever possible. The climax of the two weeks was a visit to a watchmaker's shop to see the variety of clocks and to watch the artisan at work.

Toward the end of the two weeks, the teacher again challenged her students to make a clock. For most students, the development was remarkable. Many of the students were now able to draw clocks with all the numbers in place; some attempted to add the minute markers as well.

Much can be learned from this teacher's work. She has demonstrated the diagnostic capacity of open-ended problems and has suggested ways in which teachers can monitor student progress. Most important for our purposes, she has demonstrated the power of immersing students in an environment rich in mathematics.

The math environment in a classroom—and student experiences with math—can be greatly enhanced if teachers ensure that student work is displayed. Teachers with young students often write or type the math to make it suitable for display, and the student may be given a chance to add a diagram to illustrate the work. Older students publish their own work and are challenged by the teacher to find a form of presentation that best communicates the mathematics. Often, a graph will communicate better than a string of numbers, and a diagram may replace a hundred words.

In an upper primary (ten- to twelve-year-olds) classroom we visited recently, the published mathematics included:

- Interesting number sentences.
- Responses to challenges.
- Mathematical rules that students had developed.
- Students' attempts to test these rules.
- Challenges that students had developed for others.
- Big books containing student responses to a particular challenge.
- A wide variety of polyhedra.

Teachers also need to display many kinds of adult mathematics, particularly examples of the uses of mathematics for practical purposes. Teachers are now collecting and displaying:

- Architectural plans of schools, homes, cars, work places, and household appliances.
- Maps that use a variety of scales and that have been produced for different purposes.
- Financial statements and budgets of households, school canteens, small businesses, and large corporations.
- Statistics for sporting teams, communities, and regions.
- Tables of numbers ranging from bus timetables to computer printouts.
- Diagrams that convey mathematical information.
- Demonstrations of algebra and trigonometry used to solve problems.

Adult mathematics displayed in the classroom.

- Published graphs.
- Examples of mathematics in the natural world.

Students are not expected to deal directly with these examples of adult mathematics any more than young children are expected to understand and respond to the adult conversation going on around them. But they still learn much from this immersion. They learn that adults use mathematics for important purposes and communicate it in a variety of ways. They see the symbols of the language that is mathematics and how these symbols are used to convey meaning. And they have adult models that they can begin to approximate.

Demonstration

Teachers need to take every opportunity to demonstrate math. Adults provide good models of the language of mathematics whenever they talk about mathematical ideas in context and use specialized mathematical words in association with the structure of the language. Students can themselves be useful models of mathematics if they are given opportunities to share their work with others.

In addition, students need to be familiar with the language of thinking, and teachers should regularly think out loud as one way to provide a model. Young students often hear very little of the language of thinking in their everyday environment. Adults don't think out loud very often. Parents should be encouraged to do so more frequently, and teachers need to demonstrate their thinking whenever they can. Teachers are now very consciously finding opportunities to use language such as:

- I wonder if . . .
- I expect that . . .
- If I change this . . .
- Maybe . . .
- The first thing I will try . . .

When interacting with the students, either in groups or as individuals, the teacher can ask questions that prompt the student to clarify, to hypothesize, to predict, to develop further, or to look for alternatives. The teacher models the questions that the students will ask later, either of themselves when refining their work or of others during a sharing time.

The use of mathematical conventions should be modeled, whenever appropriate, in the same way that teachers model the conventions of written language or of reading. Teachers find it useful to demonstrate, in an appropriate setting, how to use brackets to determine which operation is carried out first, how fractions are written, what exponential notation looks like (e.g., 2.3×10^3), and so on.

There are many opportunities in the classroom to demonstrate the usefulness of mathematics. Teachers can bring in examples of their own use of mathematics, from measuring for curtains to financing homes. These occasions are enriched if teachers reveal what thought processes they use. Teachers can also demonstrate the practical use of rulers, balance pans, compasses, protractors, and calculators.

Cambourne (1988, p. 34) believes that demonstrations are the raw materials of most learning, not just of learning language. Whether it is baking a cake or changing a tire, we learn easily from the many demonstrations we witness—even when they are beyond our current level of understanding—and find learning much more difficult when those demonstrations are absent. Many teachers have now reorganized their curriculum to ensure that mathematical ideas are demonstrated often—and often before the learner is expected to engage with them.

This is a dramatic departure from the traditional "Here it is, now you do it" math demonstration, a demonstration that seldom goes beyond the math the learner is required to deal with then and there. Algebra descends out of the blue with no prior warning. One month, it is all numbers, the next it is nothing but x's and y's.

We can see the inadequacies of the conventional approach to mathematics clearly by examining an example, such as negative numbers. On the one hand, we have heard secondary teachers report that they "teach" negative numbers within a few weeks, to children who have had little prior preparation. They regard it as a difficult topic and confess that a significant proportion of their students fail to master it fully. On the other hand, we have watched nine-year-olds spontaneously use negative numbers in response to the challenge:

What are the most interesting number sentences that you can write? Select the most interesting for display in the classroom.

Tim, age six, responded to this challenge with the number sentences shown in Figure 2–1. When his teacher saw him write $100 - 200 = $ M100, she asked him to read it out loud. He quickly read, "One hundred take away two hundred is minus one hundred," as if this were entirely obvious. Tim could easily calculate negative numbers but he had no symbol for them so he invented his own. The mathematical equivalent of invented spelling! Tim next wrote (incorrectly) $200 - 300 = $ M200 but after a discussion with his teacher about two take away three he changed his answer from M200 to M100. In this situation it was very easy for the teacher to observe how Tim's ideas about negative numbers were developing.

Figure 2–1. Tim's number sentences.

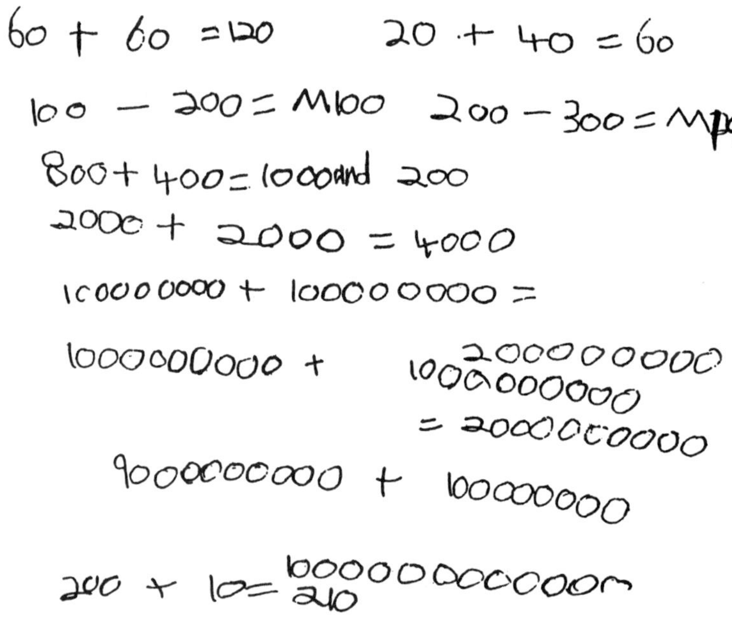

Between the two extremes—of secondary students having difficulties and a six-year-old inventing a symbol for negative numbers—there is a great void. There are few demonstrations of negative numbers in everyday life, with the possible exception of temperatures on television. Indeed there seems to be a school conspiracy to keep negative numbers hidden. All the subtraction exercises are carefully contrived to ensure positive answers. The conventional view is that primary students are not ready for negative numbers.

However, even if many of them are not ready to comprehend negative numbers fully, they certainly are ready to see them in their environment as a basis for future learning. Teachers of children as young as Tim can demonstrate negative numbers to their students, and can do so in a valid context, simply by extending the classroom number line to the left to include the numbers from −1 to −10. We are not suggesting that these teachers teach negative numbers directly. We *are* saying that negative numbers need to be

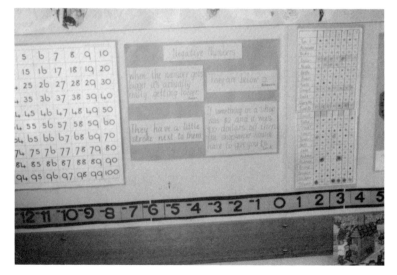

Negative numbers on a number line in a classroom of eight- and nine-year-olds.

displayed so that the children get to see the symbols that adults use and can incorporate them in their own mathematics if they choose to.

We have found that some young students will surprise us with their ability to learn complicated mathematical concepts, from negative numbers to algebra, and that exposure to these concepts will better prepare most young students to learn them later.

Engagement

Engagement with the task at hand is vital if learning is to take place. Learners continually experience demonstrations that they largely ignore. They must engage with the demonstration to learn substantially from it. Engagement will occur only if students are convinced that:

- The task is worth doing.
- The task is possible to achieve (they must see themselves as potential bike riders, writers, or mathematicians).
- There will not be any unpleasant consequences should they fail.

To ensure that engagement will occur, the teacher must pay careful attention to the mathematical tasks presented. These tasks must be both challenging and open-ended if engagement is to be maintained without the fear of failure.

One teacher of a kindergarten class (four- and five-year-olds) noted that three of her students had used subtraction informally without needing to record their answers. She

3 sugar plums.
A hand took 1
sugar plum
and got it.

Figure 2–2. A subtraction device created by a group of kindergartners.

posed this challenge: "Pretend that I don't know anything about take-aways and you have to tell me what they are." The students presented some examples, one being, "If you had three cans and one rolled away you would only have two left." The teacher then asked them to make something without using numbers to show what they meant. They returned later with the device shown in Figure 2–2, in which the hand can move through the slit and cover the plums. The teacher commented: "While the students were showing me their teaching aids, all the other children came from nowhere. They were taken with the device and started making their own."

Expectation

We expect children to be successful language users. Parents are convinced that their offspring will learn to speak, and they behave in ways that make this clear to the child. They speak to their children from birth onward and respond to their children's prespeech communications.

If adults have high expectations of all students in mathematics, value the intentions of learners, and provide challenging, open-ended activities, students develop the expectation that they will be successful learners of mathematics.

Teachers need to abandon their expectations that certain levels of mathematics apply to students in particular grade levels. Students have repeatedly astonished their teachers with the extent of their knowledge. For example, many young students have a good grasp of large numbers and ideas about infinity. Conversely, there have been many occasions when teachers assumed, wrongly, that students knew certain things because they were expected learning outcomes from structured activities or because the students were a particu-

Young students exploring a 1 to 1000 chart.

lar age. Teachers are finding that such expectations inhibit learning.

It is important that learners expect mathematics to be useful and enjoyable. They need the adults around them—particularly their parents and teachers—to have the same expectations. In addition, they need to enjoy mathematics personally and to experience its power and usefulness in their lives.

Responsibility

> Although adults play a major role in providing experiences with and models of language use and behavior, children take from those experiences and models what, how, when, and why they learn. By being able to make decisions for themselves, children gradually gain greater control over a broad set of language operations that are meaning-centered, predictive, and self-corrective and that serve each child's individual need. (Education Department of Tasmania 1987, p. 8)

Both teachers and students have responsibilities in the classroom. It is the teacher's responsibility to establish a learning environment and to set the parameters within which students may show responsibility. The teacher ensures that the learning conditions apply and that natural learning processes operate in the classroom. In addition, the teacher ensures that the student's mathematical theories are challenged. Students make decisions about what they will attend to in any learning situation and, ultimately, it is the students who are responsible for their own learning.

In language arts classes, more and more teachers are allowing students to choose what they will read, within the limitations of what is available in a particular classroom or library, while still encouraging them to attempt more challenging literature. Similarly, many teachers expect very young students to be responsible for their own writing, even in their earliest years at school; the teachers provide an interesting and challenging environment and the students decide what they wish to communicate to others. The goal—as with oral language—is to communicate meaning, and the writer must be responsible for the meanings he or she attempts to communicate. Nobody else can make our meanings for us.

Students need to be similarly responsible for their mathematics learning. We would like teachers to develop an environment in which students are naturally challenged to learn mathematics. But, in trying to do this, we immediately encounter an important difference between language and mathematics: there is no mathematical parallel to the quality literature available to students.

How much choice should a student have in selecting math work? If some language teachers are beginning to allow students to make virtually all the decisions about what they will write or read, within established limits, should it be the same in mathematics? Should students be free to choose

"As a mathematician it is your responsibility . . ."

whatever aspects of mathematics interest them? If so, how would students gain access to the full range of mathematical knowledge? The requirement to provide a balanced program, to draw student attention to certain aspects of mathematics, tends to conflict with the interests of the students and their control over their own learning.

The availability of books in the classroom allows students' writing and reading to be readily challenged, as long as they are actively writing and reading. Books provide the challenges. But books have no true mathematical parallel. That parallel would be intrinsically exciting materials produced by adults for children, materials that have an integrity and an obvious similarity to the mathematics adults enjoy. Our hope is that open-ended challenges, as described in Chapter 4 and Chapter 5, will accomplish for mathematics education what books accomplish for language. We envision libraries of these challenges, with students maintaining the responsibility for selecting from among them.

The teacher is responsible for providing challenges in the classroom. Students can challenge their own thinking,

Using mathematics in a challenging situation.

but—at least at the beginning—they need to learn how to do that by engaging with adult-produced challenges. Although teachers must ensure that student thinking is challenged in the whole range of mathematics topics considered to be important by our communities, open-ended challenges allow ultimate responsibility for what is learned to remain with the student.

Use

Students need time and appropriate contexts in which to use their developing mathematics skills, alone and with others. Having a reason to practice helps maintain relevance and engagement in the learning process. Students should be using their mathematics all the time.

Emma, age seven, was shown a practical way of deciding whether numbers were odd or even by arranging them into two rows of Unifix™ cubes. She was then asked to investigate which numbers were odd and which were even. She worked systematically through the numbers, recording them as odd or even (Figure 2–3). She practiced counting, adding, and recording numbers over an extended period.

Emma was so motivated to use her mathematical skills in the context of an activity that was interesting to her and where the successful use of her skills mattered that she happily went far beyond what her teacher expected, finding the odd and even numbers up to 101. Incidentally, it was no surprise that Emma could formulate the following rule for odd and even numbers:

They both go in two's—odd [numbers] start with one, even [numbers] start with two.

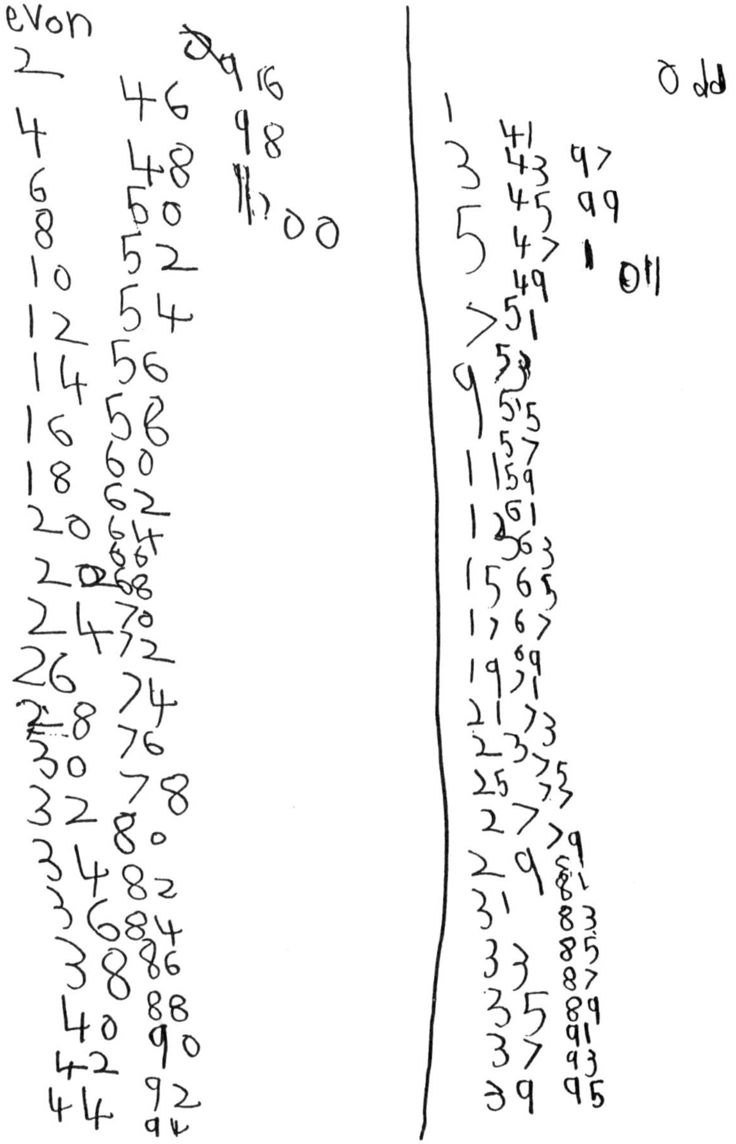

even

2
4
6
8
10
12
14
16
18
20
22
24
26
28
30
32
34
36
38
40
42
44

46
48
50
52
54
56
58
60
62
64
66
68
70
72
74
76
78
80
82
84
86
88
90
92
94

96
98
100

Odd

1
3
5
7
9
11
13
15
17
19
21
23
25
27
29
31
33
35
37
39

41
43
45
47
49
51
53
55
57
59
61
63
65
67
69
71
73
75
77
79
81
83
85
87
89
91
93
95

97
99
101

Figure 2–3.   Emma's chart of odd and even numbers.

Approximation

Adults warmly accept the very approximate efforts of young children as they make their first attempts at learning to talk. There is absolutely no expectation that the "correct" or adult model will be used. If there were, children would probably never learn to speak. What the adult does expect is that the child will convey meaning. The child says "Dat cup me?" and the adult replies, "Yes, you can have that cup," modeling the conventional form, usually in an approving voice.

Similarly, young children approximate mathematically. The child counts "One, two, three, seven, ten," and the adult, pleased that the first three numbers were in order, replies, "Yes dear, that's good counting," and proceeds to say the numbers in their conventional order. Children write numbers, often mixed up with letters and other symbols, as they experiment with what they see adults doing, and adults are pleased by these attempts.

Cambourne (1988) believes that the willingness to accept approximations is essential for language learning, because it sets in process a cycle of hypothesis testing that is analogous to what we call theory refinement (this is discussed in Chapter 3). If refinement processes are to operate in classrooms, teachers must be willing to accept approximations as the basis for future refinement.

The ability to estimate approximate answers is a vitally important part of mathematics. Students need to be able to estimate and approximate in order to check their calculations. This is particularly true when calculators and computers are used, because it's so easy to unknowingly press the wrong keys. It is essential that students be able to check the calculator through approximations.

Teachers are now making major efforts to teach students how to approximate, but they are often unsuccessful. The difficulties arise from the manner in which the vast majority of school math is presented to students—that is, in closed questions such as $9 - 3 = ?$ It is hard to accept approximations when closed questions are used. The answer is simply right or wrong. The end result of answering right/wrong questions year after year is that students learn not to approximate; if it's not absolutely right, it's wrong.

Teachers have found that they can readily accept student responses as approximations if they present the mathematics as open-ended questions or challenges. These have no one "right" answer, so the difficulties with right/wrong questions are avoided.

Language teachers help students understand that learning is not copied correctness and that risk taking—approximating—is part of the process of learning to make and convey meaning. In such an environment, students are willing to be risk takers. Initially, many teachers find this hard to transfer to the mathematics area. It can be a problem for both teachers and students (particularly older students) and usually is associated with their previous experiences with the subject and their established beliefs about the nature of mathematics. However, the creation of a supportive environment that allows students (and teachers) to become risk takers will enable them to experiment with mathematical ideas and with ways of communicating these developing ideas. As students refine their thinking and powers of communication, they move toward adult models.

Response

Students need nonthreatening responses to their developing ideas about mathematics and their attempts to convey their thinking. The responses should value the intention of the student rather than focus on the deficits. However, this does not preclude either asking questions aimed at further clarification or modeling back to the student the use of the conventional form.

Teachers can respond to the meaning in students' mathematical communications, model correct forms if appropriate, and provide support for further development. Students need encouragement and feedback about their attempts to use mathematics, and it is important that opportunities are created to share mathematical experiences with both peers and with caring adults. It is also important that teachers challenge students to further refine their mathematical ideas.

Teachers have found that they can establish these natural learning conditions in their mathematics classrooms. The end result is a major change in both their teaching and their students' learning.

Chapter Three

Natural Learning Processes

W e have described, in Chapter 2, the conditions for natural learning and how teachers have used them for mathematics. The question now is: How does learning occur once those conditions have been established? That is, what are the learning processes that operate naturally when the appropriate conditions are in place?

We don't yet have definitive answers to these questions; we simply have not observed enough math classrooms to fully understand what happens. We can draw to some degree from the work with language learners, but, with the possible exception of the teaching of writing, this work has not been fully explicit about processes.

Frank Smith (1975) and others have described natural learning as a process by which learners improve their theories. Smith believes that learners improve their cognitive structures, or theories, by a four-stage process that involves (a) generating a hypothesis, (b) testing the hypothesis, (c) evaluating feedback, and (d) confirming or rejecting the hypothesis (p. 125).

Smith says that learners "test whether their hypotheses are good by putting them to work. . . . They conduct experiments" (p. 126). In other words, learners test their theories by trying them out in the world and refining them.

Cambourne (1988, pp. 38–39) also describes a hypothesis-testing cycle, while Dyson (1982) refers to children's "solving the written language puzzle" (p. 829). Holdaway (1979, p. 96) writes about a hypothesis-testing model and relates it to the natural rhythms of challenge followed by confirmation or self-correction, which in turn leads to a relaxation of tension and provides intrinsic rewards. He writes, "The rhythm of challenge, effort and reward is so fundamental to learning—indeed to every few seconds of human endeavour—that to overlook it is to invite failure" (p. 97).

Our view is that natural learning proceeds via a variety of processes that connect thought (our theories) and action in cyclic fashion. For this to happen, the natural learning conditions must be operating. With Holdaway, we believe that these processes are fueled by challenging situations and the rewards that flow from meeting the challenges.

The natural learning cycle

Cambourne describes the cycle as being "a common observation in the learning to talk context" (1986, p. 20). This is what he calls a "hypothesise, testing, modify hypothesis, test again" cycle (1988, p. 38). A learner selects and interprets information that leads to a hypothesis. This is tested by the learner's "having a go," which results in feedback that the attempt is not quite conventional. This, in turn, leads to puzzlement (intelligent unrest). As a result, the learner modifies the hypothesis, learning occurs, and the cycle continues.

Our natural learning cycle, diagramed in Figure 3–1, can be seen as a generalization of those processes described by Cambourne and Smith, but expressed in our language of theory refinement. We call the processes linking theory to practice *testing* and those connecting action to thought *reflecting*. Some of the processes involved in natural learning are:

Testing processes—from thought to action: playing (with equipment or materials, etc.), exploring, planning, testing, investigating, making, designing.

Reflecting processes—from action to thought: reflecting, monitoring, making a model, collecting feedback, hypothesizing, sharing or explaining, discriminating (selecting and rejecting), conferring, editing, publishing.

The lists are neither exhaustive nor mutually exclusive. For example, investigating how something works may at

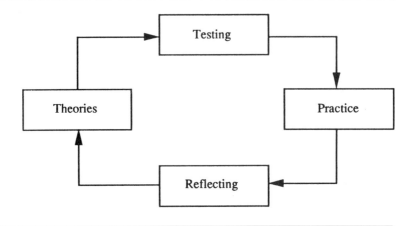

Figure 3–1. *The natural learning cycle.*

times be a reflective process. The processes are listed here to provide a model of the processes to look for in the classroom and the type of processes to foster. In the next sections, we describe a few of these processes in more detail.

Testing theories

It is natural for most of us to test our theories by seeing how they work in practice. When confronted with a new piece of equipment or a new medium, we approach it with initial theories derived from past experiences or prior knowledge. Our initial reaction is often to play or explore. We push the buttons to see what happens. We fiddle with the bits and pieces to see what we can do with them. We explore the new material, perhaps use it to make something, and start to find out what we can do with it.

As learners refine their ideas, new questions arise. Often they come from attempts to apply existing theories to more-general situations or to explore the limits of the theory. New theory refinement cycles come into operation as the theory is tested in these ways.

Planning

Planning is a useful way to move from theory to practice. People plan quite naturally, although sometimes it is not easy to be explicit about what is being attempted.

We have observed that planning is more likely to follow initial playing. As learners come to understand better what is involved in a particular challenge, they are better able to formulate a strategy to help them proceed further.

Teachers often find it useful to build an initial stage into an activity in which students can play around with and explore the new situation before they formulate a plan. With older students, the plan may then be formally recorded. Sometimes it is helpful to allow students to share their planning ideas. That way, students who find it difficult to get started have a variety of approaches available to them. Joint planning, in the form of brainstorming with the whole class or group, often allows a variety of ideas to come forward. One idea may spark a train of thought with other students, and a more sophisticated response to the challenge may result.

We have previously referred to this initial preplanning or planning stage as structuring the challenge. In most good challenges, it is not entirely obvious what students should do. Students of all ages may need support to understand just what the challenge means. That support may come in the form of hearing how other people respond. The support of a group, and the teacher, may be necessary so that students don't fail by simply not beginning.

We believe that teachers should give whatever support is necessary in the early stages of a challenge, as long as they don't take over the activity from the students.

Making

Making something is an excellent way of connecting thought with action. Many of the best challenges involve making. We have already mentioned several such challenges—make a clock, make a pattern, make a ruler, make triangles with big angles in them. We have found challenges that ask students to make their own measuring instruments to be particularly valuable: The students test theories about how the measuring device works, analyze what is being measured and what units to use, and investigate what conventional devices— such as balances—actually do. Figure 3–2 shows the angle measurer that Mathew, age nine, produced in response to this sort of challenge.

The challenges work best if students are given reasons for using their own measuring devices. They might be asked which lengths they can measure easily with their rulers and

Figure 3–2. Mathew's angle measurer.

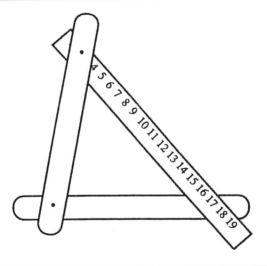

which are difficult. Older students might be asked to use their angle-of-elevation measurer to find out how the angle changes with distance from an object. By using their instruments in open-ended situations, students get feedback on the degree of success of their endeavor. We believe that these experiences open students' eyes to the conventional devices. They see them more clearly and learn about them as a result.

It is important that students have opportunities to make various shapes and solid figures with a range of properties, so that they develop a feel for the very different shapes that can be made. This may include making triangles, quadrilaterals, or other geometric shapes with the same perimeter or area, or polyhedra with a fixed surface area or volume.

Investigating

Investigations are becoming increasingly popular in math classrooms. The idea of investigation is fundamental both to the study of mathematics and to an understanding of the ways in which mathematics can be used to extend knowledge and solve problems in many fields (Cockcroft 1982).

There is considerable overlap between the notion of investigation and our concept of challenge. Many investigations are good challenges, while most challenges require students to perform some investigation. Some investigations are, however, quite closed. Take this example from the *NCTM Standards* (1989): "Cut a 12-by-16-cm rectangle on a diagonal as shown. What geometric shapes can you make? Which one has the shortest perimeter?" (p. 34). Closed investigations may not be a difficulty if the teacher establishes a classroom in which learning from the investigation is valued, rather than obtaining "the answer." Otherwise, such an investigation can result in feelings of dissatisfaction and failure when students fail to find the "right" answer. Again, we stress the importance of establishing the natural learning conditions so that students know that positive consequences will follow when they take risks.

Reflective processes

In a theory refinement approach, it is essential that students be involved in reflective processes. We have mentioned approximation as a necessary condition to allow reflection and refinement to occur, and we have discussed the role of open-ended challenges in initiating and supporting such processes.

In mathematics, we hope that students will refine both their theories and their presentations of them. When students communicate their responses to a challenge—by writing, displaying calculations, drawing diagrams, plotting graphs, or just talking about the mathematics—they often are refining their mathematical communications. At the same time, they may be refining their thinking.

Discriminating (Selection and Rejection)

Part of learning in any subject is learning how to discriminate between good and bad, quality and trash. In mathematics, the emphasis has traditionally been on getting the correct answer, with little if any emphasis on other aspects. We have mentioned before that students need to learn the aesthetics of mathematics: what makes a mathematical solution elegant, what is exciting mathematically, and what about mathematics is fun. Instead of being fed a monoalgorithmic diet, students need to be able to explore the different algorithms and be able to select the approach best suited to particular circumstances.

Good challenges require students to discriminate. It might simply be to select the most interesting number sentence to publish. It might be to decide which is the most useful measuring instrument for particular circumstances. Sometimes the requirement is to select a suitable means of communicating the results.

Teachers can ensure that refinement processes operate by ensuring that challenges provide reasons for students to discriminate. They can initiate and encourage discussions on the aesthetics of mathematics and the effectiveness of different approaches to a challenge. They can encourage students to pursue aspects of mathematics they enjoy. Most important, they can provide models of people who themselves enjoy mathematics, who use it in their own lives, and who appreciate its wider qualities.

Teachers can foster reflection in ways modeled on the process approach to writing. The writing process includes conferencing, editing, and publishing. Teachers have developed mathematical analogues to all of these and they are described in the next sections.

Sharing and Conferring

Students readily share their mathematical experiences with others. In the classroom, this may involve a formal sharing time at the end of a session, conferring with the teacher or other students, or simply explaining the mathematics to someone else. The sharing may include descriptions of what was investigated, how the investigation was carried out, what was noticeable or interesting, and which aspects could be investigated further.

Students can also easily be encouraged to verbalize their thinking about a particular bit of mathematics. This reveals a student's specific ideas, and the teacher can then ask pertinent questions and provide meaningful examples that will extend, or challenge, the student's thinking. The act of verbalizing thinking is valuable as reflection; it often assists in clarifying thinking, and other students benefit from hearing how others think. In this way, sharing and conferencing become an integral part of theory refinement.

Here's one instance in which math conferencing helped a student: A teacher of eight- to ten-year-olds was using activity cards to introduce the idea of fractions. Students were asked to divide some pictured objects into halves,

A student shares her findings with the whole class.

thirds, and so on. Next they were challenged to draw some objects of their own, similarly divided into equal parts.

Thomas drew a banana divided into four sections as shown in Figure 3–3. Looking over Thomas's shoulder, the teacher asked if Thomas thought the banana had been divided into four equal bits. Thomas could see that the left-hand piece was smaller than the others, so his teacher challenged him to find a way to divide the banana into four equal quarters.

Some time later, when Thomas had made no further progress, we asked the teacher what she would do in a language class if a student reached a dead end. She explained that the student would be asked to confer with other students. The student would explain what had been done so far and the other students would make suggestions.

Thomas decided to conference about the banana challenge. Because conferring was already a regular classroom activity, Thomas knew exactly how to proceed. He sought out another student and explained what he was trying to do. Together, they came up with an improved solution, slicing the banana lengthwise.

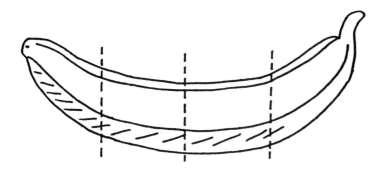

Figure 3–3. A banana as divided into sections by Thomas.

This example illustrates a number of important features. First, the teacher kept the challenge open and refused to give a "correct" answer when the student could not proceed further; also, the responsibility for learning was left with the student, who acted to get the help he needed; finally, by conferring, the student had to explain the situation to a friend, thus increasing the amount of language used and, we hope, giving him a better understanding of the problem.

Editing

Part of the process of becoming an independent learner is taking the responsibility to check, revise, refine, and perhaps develop one's work. In language, many teachers have made this quite explicit, placing the responsibility for editing with the students. In some schools, the teachers and students have made wall charts with suggestions to enhance the editing process. These teachers found it a simple matter to do the same for mathematics and the students readily made suggestions about what to include on the charts.

The language area has such resources as dictionaries, word lists, and other reference materials to support editing. If students are to be more independent in editing their mathematics work, it is necessary to have math resources available.

Procedures for editing mathematics, jointly developed by the teacher and her class and displayed as a list for students to refer to.

Such resources could include calculators, wall charts with the numbers 1 through 100 (and beyond), number lines, math dictionaries, and class-made books.

Publishing

The writing process involves the selection of written work to publish for a wider audience. This published work must be attractively presented and clearly written, and the conventions of written language need to be followed. A similar process can be used effectively for mathematics, although a sense of audience is sometimes a bit more difficult to develop.

Mathematics publishing also involves selection and presentation. Students are encouraged to reflect on their work and select the best to publish. Effective presentation may require the use of diagrams, tables, or graphs. And publication demonstrates to students that calculations are easier for others to understand when they are set out clearly. So, students have a reason to check their calculations and refine them if necessary.

Some of the teachers we've worked with have stolen an idea from reading—a "wheel of ideas"—to help students refine their work for publication. The wheel is a list of suggestions that have been developed by students and teachers together. The ideas have been arranged on a wheel with a pointer. Students spin the wheel, and a suitable activity is indicated:

Would you like to share your results with a friend?

Are there better ways of recording your results?

Do you wish to publish your results?

Are your calculations correct? Check any you are not sure about.

How can you make what you have found out even more interesting?

Ask a "What would happen if———" question.

Can you make an even more difficult response to the challenge?

Think up some new challenges related to what you have done.

Write a similar challenge for a friend.

Could you improve your results using a calculator?

Is there some aspect of the challenge you would like to research further?

Write a list of instructions someone else could follow to do what you have done.

Write to———[a teacher, friend, etc.] describing how you feel about the challenge.

Draw a diagram, map, or picture that illustrates your results.

Write a number sentence or story about what you found out.

Make a model to show your results.

Write a TV or newspaper advertisement based on your findings.

Would it work if you changed———[a variable]?

Write to the teacher, describing how this challenge could be improved.

To sum up: In natural learning, learners try out their developing mathematical theories in practical situations and refine their theories as a result of what happens. Both theory and practice—mathematical ideas and their applications—are developed together. Theory refinement happens best when teachers ensure that the natural learning conditions are in operation and when students are presented with challenges sufficiently open-ended to allow their emerging ideas to be tested and refined.

Chapter Four

Open-Ended Challenges

The need for quality is well established in language teaching. Teachers have realized that feeding students a constant diet of second-rate literature will produce second-rate writers. Teachers are now insisting that students be immersed in quality literature to develop their aesthetic sensibilities and to provide models of quality writing.

To date there has been little consideration of quality in math classrooms. Students are not expected to develop any sensibilities about good mathematics beyond getting the correct answer. For those who continue with the subject in college, it can come as a shock to find that getting the correct answer is not enough.

Teachers who want their students to develop a sense of and respect for quality mathematics must present those students with mathematical situations that:

- Are meaningful entities, not fragments isolated as exercises.
- Incorporate multiple approaches to solving any given problem.
- Emphasize problems that have no single correct answer, no single correct procedure, so that students can learn to discriminate between possible approaches and solutions.
- Have been produced with quality and designed to interest learners.

Within the context of these situations, teachers must:

- Discuss the quality of different pieces of mathematics or different approaches.
- Invite students to select the best of their work for communication to others (i.e., provide avenues for students to publish their work).
- Give students the opportunity to reflect on the quality of their own work and how they can improve it.

One way to allow quality to become an important part of school mathematics is to present open-ended problems or challenges. We believe that challenges have the potential to become for mathematics what books are for language learning.

We realized early in our project that conventionally presented mathematics questions and problems would not allow natural conditions to be established or desirable processes to operate. We began to use open-ended problems or challenges to help resolve these difficulties. (We prefer to call them challenges because of the negative connotations of the word "problem." If you have a problem, you are in trouble, and we prefer to regard mathematics as challenging.)

Conventional mathematics questions look like this:

$7 + 5 = ?$
Solve the equation $x^2 + 5x + 6 = 0$

Such questions are characterized by having a right answer. We say they are closed. It is almost impossible to use a natural learning approach if closed questions are the sole means for presenting mathematics to students. Conventional math questions are posed by the teacher, sometimes via a textbook; the correct answer is also supplied by the teacher or the text. The students are trying to reproduce the teacher's (or book's) thinking, rather than taking responsibility for thinking for themselves. Also, it is difficult for teachers to accept approximations when student responses are judged either right or wrong. Hence, natural learning conditions of approximation and responsibility are difficult to establish in the classroom if closed questions predominate.

As a result of our work in classrooms and discussions with teachers, we learned that other Tasmanian curriculum development projects had circumvented the difficulties associated with closed questions in interesting ways. The Arts in Education Project had developed an approach to art education that emphasized learning processes (Felton and

68

Open—Ended Challenges

Coman 1986). To initiate and support these processes, teachers were using open-ended problems or challenges. In a typical introductory challenge in the visual arts, students are provided with some stimulus material, such as a piece of dry seaweed, and then told:

> Draw different lines you can see in the seaweed.
> Select the sort of lines you like best and use them to represent the seaweed.

In addition, we found a science project for ten- to fourteen-year-olds that used open-ended problems (Education Department of Tasmania 1988). Students, and teachers, were being challenged by problems like these:

> How could you make this trolley move without touching it?

> How could you make a peg fall more slowly?

So we asked teachers to try some math challenges with their students, and they found that open-ended challenges were critical to establishing natural learning conditions in the classroom. These challenges allowed students to use the full range of their mathematical capabilities without fear of getting a wrong answer. There are no wrong answers! Teachers could accept a student's initial response as an approximation and respond constructively. Open-ended challenges also shifted responsibility for learning to the students. The *learners* decide what is meaningful to them and develop appropriate responses.

A first challenge

Despite all these inherent advantages, we initially had great difficulty in building open-ended challenges for mathematics. We are so conditioned to mathematics problems having a right answer! Fortunately, we found one to get us started:

> What are the most interesting number sentences you can write? Select the most interesting for display in the classroom.

As teachers tried this challenge in their classrooms, they noticed some interesting consequences. First, nobody got it wrong! For the first time, whole classes were working on the same math question without a single failure. Teachers found they could accept student work simply as interesting number sentences.

Of course, there were often computation errors that needed correction before the work could be displayed. But students worked to refine and improve the quality of their work, checking calculations and stretching themselves to produce even more interesting work. They would then reflect on their work and select the most interesting number sentences for display.

Challenges are diagnostic

Teachers discovered that some students were capable of doing mathematics far beyond that being taught. One nine-year-old, for example, was determined to get a square root into his interesting number sentence. Others surprised their teachers by working with negative numbers. On the other hand, teachers found students who didn't properly understand the mathematics they were presumed to know.

In other words, challenges are diagnostic. They help teachers find out what students know, what is challenging, and what sort of work would be appropriate in the future.

Teachers found that students respond to challenges at their own level of development. Instead of the teacher's needing to individualize the work, as with conventional mathematics, students do it for themselves. This is a boon to any teacher facing the daunting task of trying to individualize the work for thirty students. A relatively small number of challenges can replace piles of work cards.

Here is an example of the power of challenges. Mathew, age nine, was the student who was determined to get a square root into his number sentence. He multiplied 16 by 16 on the side of his page, producing 256 as the target number so that his last operation could be a square root. He then wrote "3 + 9 − 0 ÷ 0.5" to start his equation. Asked what the result was so far, he answered, "Twenty-four." Next, he began dividing 24 into 256. He explained to his friend that he would do this by a complicated process resembling subtraction, rather than by long division. When he sensed that his result was not correct, he decided to estimate the answer.

A little later he had written:

$$\sqrt{3 + 9 - 0 \div 0.5 \times 10.25} = 16$$

When asked about the 10.25, he explained that he was not sure if it should be that or 10.75. Further discussion revealed that he was trying to express his remainder as a decimal.

Mathew's teacher asked him if he would like to publish a version of his interesting number sentence. The refining process was in place for the class's language work, so Mathew knew what to do. In fact, Mathew worked on his sentence on several occasions over the next few days, revising and improving it.

This activity showed a great deal about Mathew's mathematical knowledge. For example he could divide by 0.5 and could carry out operations from left to right. However, he was unaware of the conventional order of operations (divi-

Challenge: Find two objects that are heavier than the blackboard eraser but lighter than your shoe.

sion and multiplication before addition and subtraction). He understood square roots as the reverse operation to squaring. He was ready to learn more about division and to be introduced to long division.

Mathew's teacher was very impressed by the mathematics he produced. She commented, "I was not sure how to set challenging enough work for Mathew before, but now I see that if the questions are open-ended, he will challenge himself."

Creativity shines through

One of our most exciting discoveries was the creativity unleashed by open-ended challenges. For example, we issued this challenge:

Make something to measure with. Use it to find out what it measures best.

It has been a delight to watch students develop all sorts of creative measuring tapes and to see others spontaneously start constructing something for measuring angles.

One teacher varied the challenge:

Make something to measure how much rain has fallen.

A six-year-old girl made a cardboard strip with the numbers 1 to 10 on it and placed it in a large paper plate with the 1 in the center. As the rain would fall, she explained, the pool of water in the plate would widen and the numbers would measure the increase.

Much of the student work included in this book shows just how creative children are in open-ended mathematical situations. Mathew's angle measurer (Figure 3–2) is a creative response to measuring angles, Tim invented a suitable symbol for negative numbers when he needed to (Figure 2–1), while Abigail's hand (Figure 2–2), is a delightful representation of a "take-away" situation.

Challenges teach

We have found that challenges should be directed at specific areas of the curriculum. They are not just interesting activities or investigations for their own sake. They teach students about specific mathematical concepts. The challenge "Make triangles with big angles in them. What is the biggest angle you can make in a triangle?" is designed to help students learn that there are 180 degrees in the three angles of a triangle and in a straight line (straight angle).

Teachers use challenges in a variety of ways. Some start with an occasional challenge, use more challenges as they reassure themselves that their students are still learning, and finally replace most of their conventional mathematics activities with challenges. Others just include a few challenges in the curriculum to provide a change of pace.

Even teachers who use a lot of challenges continue to use other approaches as well. Many will conduct a session of whole-class mental arithmetic at the start of their mathematics work, perhaps based on the suggestions of Alistair McIntosh (1980). Others may provide times in which students develop their skills with quite closed calculations (although the students can still be asked to design their own exercises).

At the start of the year, and at the start of new topics, a teacher will probably want to use very open and diagnostic challenges. An open challenge can be issued to the whole class. For number work, for example, the students can be challenged to write interesting number sentences. Then, as the teacher learns what particular students can and cannot do, the challenges can become more specific.

When challenges are issued to the whole class, the teacher can act as scribe while the students suggest various strategies and proceed to open up lines of investigation. Whole-class challenges are an important means of demonstrating to students a variety of ways of tackling a challenge, recording and displaying data, and so on.

Other times, challenges should be issued to small groups for whom the teacher feels they are appropriate. The teacher assesses the student work (often informally, with notes in a record book) and decides what is likely to challenge the student further.

Most teachers start a challenge by giving the class, or group, an opportunity to talk together about the challenge. Often, it is not obvious where to start a particular challenge. Students may need clarification of the language involved (e.g., What are consecutive numbers?) and it is usually helpful if the teacher lists student suggestions about strategies. We refer to these initial stages as structuring the challenge. Occasionally, a student may not be able to find a starting point at all and the teacher may have to narrow the focus.

Most teachers end their sessions by inviting the students to share their work with the rest of the class. The students outline their procedures and explain what they plan to do next. The group comments and offers suggestions, which serves to provide support, encourage reflection and meaning making, and challenge individuals to go further.

Class presentations may be new to young students, who are not familiar with recording and presenting mathematical information. One primary teacher begins by asking the students to share their discoveries orally. She records the responses on the board and then demonstrates different ways of recording and presenting the information, using such tools as diagrams, tables, or graphs. Provided with this model, the children became increasingly versatile in choosing the appropriate way to publish their work.

Some teachers regularly schedule time to demonstrate some aspect of mathematics to their students. Demonstrations are usually associated with a real-life event or something that is fun to explore. Since these demonstrations are often beyond the students' current levels of operation, they serve to prepare the students for future activities.

Remember that challenges can be used more than once with the same group of students, to show development in their understanding. Each time students try the challenge, they will take it further. When the challenge is no longer challenging, however, its usefulness is exhausted.

Finally, challenges are fun. Students enjoy mathematics when it is presented via challenges. They often work for extended periods of time for the satisfaction inherent in meeting a challenge. Sessions may run as long as an hour or an hour and a half, so be flexible!

Teachers like teaching this way, too. They find, just as students do, that they become more interested in math when they view it as a challenge.

Chapter Five

Designing Challenges

*I*t was difficult at first to generate open-ended problems for mathematics. However, once we moved into the new mind set, it rapidly became straightforward. We now see a number of principles that can be used to design challenges relevant to any area of the mathematics curriculum.

Let the students decide the numbers

The challenge to write interesting number sentences can be generalized to apply to almost any component of the curriculum. All that is required, in many instances, is simply to allow students to decide for themselves what numbers they will use in their mathematics. The students then take more of an ownership role in the activities, and the teacher learns what numbers the students can work with and where the starting point for refinement should be.

The simple number sentence challenge can be adapted in a variety of ways. Students can be challenged to write number sentences that:

- Include both division and multiplication.
- Have the number 12 as the answer.
- Have big numbers in them.
- Involve subtraction.
- Require a calculator.
- Use fractions (and a fraction strip or similar prop).
- Involve the squares of numbers.
- Are true for any numbers.

The possibilities are infinite.

Many conventional activities can be converted into challenges, as demonstrated in Chapter 1 by the teacher who asked her class to prepare their own catalogue offering various discounts. Similar techniques can be used to present virtually the entire number curriculum, across all grade levels, in open-ended ways. Of course it is important to ensure that writing number sentences doesn't become too routine, or hackneyed, for students. Teachers should use interesting and challenging approaches to open up the number work. Looking for patterns is one way.

Patterns, rules, and validity

Looking for patterns is a fundamental activity in mathematics. Some would say it is *the* fundamental mathematical procedure. And it is very open-ended.

Young children need to be challenged to look for patterns in many contexts. This includes making repeating patterns of their own with a wide variety of materials, with numbers, and with different sensory mediums. It also includes identifying patterns and transforming patterns from one form to another (e.g., turning a color pattern into a sound pattern). Much of the work that primary teachers already do with patterns is quite open-ended. Here are some examples:

Make repeating patterns using colors that you like. Make a number pattern that repeats in exactly the same way as your best color pattern. Publish what you have made.

Experiment with different sounds until you find three sounds that you like. Make different repeating patterns using your three sounds. Select the pattern you like best and record it on paper, using a different color to represent each sound.

Make a repeating pattern that you like out of blocks. Sit back to back with a friend so that she can't see your pattern. Tell her how to make a pattern just the same as yours.

Start with 0 and add 5s. Use the calculator if you wish. This is the 5 times table. What patterns can you find in the table? Select the most interesting and display it.

Pattern finding should not be restricted to younger students. Older students can look for patterns in all areas of math—in square numbers, in sums of numbers (even, odd, and consecutive), and so on. Students can look for patterns in

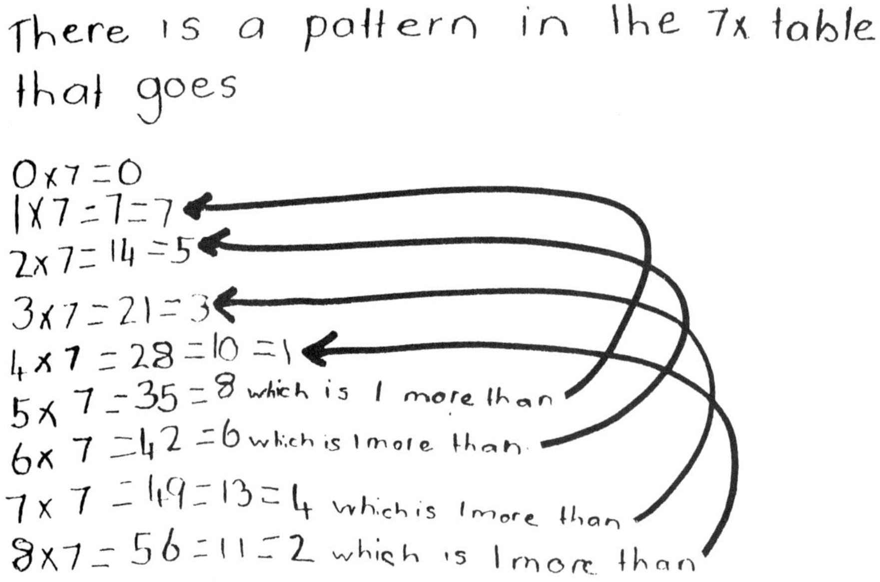

Figure 5–1. The pattern found by Georgia in the 7 times table.

There is a pattern in the 7x table that goes

$0 \times 7 = 0$
$1 \times 7 = 7 = 7$
$2 \times 7 = 14 = 5$
$3 \times 7 = 21 = 3$
$4 \times 7 = 28 = 10 = 1$
$5 \times 7 = 35 = 8$ which is 1 more than
$6 \times 7 = 42 = 6$ which is 1 more than
$7 \times 7 = 49 = 13 = 4$ which is 1 more than
$8 \times 7 = 56 = 11 = 2$ which is 1 more than

plane figures, in their relationships (triangles in four- or five-sided figures) and angular properties. They can investigate patterns in their measurements of lengths, perimeters, areas, masses, and capacities.

A class of ten-year-olds, for example, investigated the patterns that they could find in different tables. Jo found that the last digit in the 6 times table went 6, 2, 8, 4, 0 and then repeated, while Joel found that the 4 times table was double the 2 times table. Georgia decided to investigate the 7 times table and to the surprise of her teacher found the pattern shown in Figure 5–1. Georgia found the pattern by adding the digits of the numbers in the table, something she had investigated previously, and observing that the resulting number four places further down the table increased by one.

Georgia was using a lot of mathematics. She was improving her familiarity with the 7 times table at the same time as she multiplied and added and practiced looking for patterns. All this was accompanied by the delight of making a valuable discovery on her own. As Georgia and her classmates become more aware of the patterns generated by adding digits, particularly in tables (the 9 times table gives a very interesting pattern), her teacher might ask them to consider why these particular patterns appear. The students might also be encouraged to express their patterns as rules and to suggest why the rules work. One example of a pattern expressed as a rule is shown in Figure 5–2.

Even young students should occasionally be challenged to see whether they can express any of their patterns as a rule or theory. This is one reason for emphasizing patterns in mathematics; they help us develop generalized rules that we can use to understand and to predict. It is important, however, that students not be placed in a position where there is just one rule to be found and the teacher is pushing for its discovery. One way to avoid that trap is to establish an understanding that, wherever possible, the students (and the teacher) will attempt to turn a pattern into a rule.

Once a rule or theory has been proposed, test its validity.

Figure 5–2. Beth's rule based on the pattern she observed in adding even and odd numbers.

Rule testing is not just a simple matter of proving theorems, as many mathematical textbooks would have us believe. In mathematics, rule testing is a continuous, open-ended activity. No theorems are ever safe from attack and the need for refinement. We can never be sure that the assumptions underlying any proof are adequate or consistent; we cannot be certain that we have not overlooked some step in the proof or that some new mathematical discovery will not force us to reconceptualize our ideas. The history of mathematics is littered with examples of "proved" proofs that have been found wanting (Lakatos 1976).

We need to include theory testing as an integral part of school mathematics. We should also present proofs to students for examination. They may be the work of other students, our own rough proofs, or textbook theorems. The challenge may simply be, "What can you find out about this?"

Earlier, we saw twelve-year-olds investigating a challenge built around four consecutive numbers (see page 12). One student noticed that the sum of the first and last number equaled the sum of the middle two numbers. He finally reported that he could understand why the rule worked. He explained,

> Because the numbers are consecutive the second number is one more than the first and the third is one less than the last. So if you add the first and last numbers you will get exactly the same as adding the second and third. So adding the four numbers will be the same as twice the sum of the first and last numbers.

His proof was published for other students to examine and some started to adapt the proof for rules involving other sums of consecutive numbers.

Recognizing patterns, formulating rules, and testing rules should be activities in all mathematics classrooms.

In many ways, these activities make for truly mathematical study. However, we are not advocating a discovery approach to mathematics teaching and learning in which students have to reinvent important mathematical ideas. That is not a natural learning approach at all. We can expose young children to complicated language and adult ideas in a way that still leaves the learner with the responsibility for dealing with these words and ideas.

Teachers and students can have a lot of fun with challenges that start with "Some people say . . ." or some variant ("My friend says . . ."; "Miss Williams says . . ."; "My rule is . . ."; "I read in a book that . . ."). By using such challenges, teachers are confronting students with important mathematical discoveries in a way that leaves the student, not the teacher, responsible for the learning. The basic challenge in all of these expressions is, "What can you find out about this?"

It is often best to present only part of the rule or expression. For example, providing the consecutive number challenge for just four numbers allows students to extend the rule to other groups of numbers, to generalize it.

Sometimes it is important to present rules that are false or in need of refinement. Otherwise, students will come to accept them as always true and they will likely to be less analytical. Hershel's method of finding a fraction between two given fractions (NCTM 1989, p. 230) would make an interesting challenge. Hershel said that $\frac{3}{6}$ was between $\frac{2}{5}$ and $\frac{4}{7}$ because 3 is between 2 and 4 and 6 is between 5 and 7. The activity could be simply opened out by expressing the challenge as:

What can you find out about Hershel's rule? Explain your most interesting finding to a friend.

For some students, finding examples and counterexamples might be enough. Others will want to investigate why some work and others don't and start to refine Hershel's rule.

Here's another challenge:

> John Wise, a friend of mine, says that the area of a
> circle is three times the radius squared. What can you
> find out about this? Write a letter to John, explaining
> what you have found.

Some students respond by trying to determine more accurate values for pi. This is a challenge that still occupies adult mathematicians!

Math education journals are a good source of rules for use in challenges. One we like is:

> Brian Resnick (a seventh grader) is reported
> [Fromewick 1988] to have discovered that the square
> root of 25 plus the square root of 16 is 9, which is the
> same as 25 − 16. What can you find out about Brian's
> discovery?

Focus on process

If teachers focus on the process, rather than the answer, even closed activities become more open, simply because there are many ways of solving any particular problem. However, students are so used to focusing on correct answers that they are often unwilling to believe a teacher who emphasizes processes. Cobb, Wood, and Yackel (1990) describe a classroom in which a teacher has cultivated a conjecturing atmosphere. The teacher had to be quite explicit in both word and action to communicate that she valued thinking more than answers. She capitalized on classroom situations in which students presented an incorrect response by using them to illustrate her expectations that students could share their thinking without penalty.

Another way to shift the emphasis to process is to use "process language" in the design of activities—words such as *explore, investigate, make, design, create,* and *publish* are ideal for challenges and almost always result in open-ended activities.

Finally, we must emphasize that in developing a challenge the focus should be on the mathematics that the student is learning. Challenges are not just interesting activities to keep students busy. They must be designed so that students come to deal with the particular aspects of mathematics that they need to learn about.

Student challenges

Young children love to challenge themselves. They attempt to count to ever bigger numbers, to build ever more elaborate constructions; they love to use big numbers in calculations; discussions about infinity arise in primary classrooms as the children push their emerging understandings further and further. In conventional schooling, that love often is lost as students gradually come to rely on the teacher as the source of learning tasks. However, as teachers expect and encourage students to challenge themselves, as teachers demonstrate good challenges and explain why some are better than others, as teachers accept student questions as starting points, they will discover that their students take more responsibility for their own learning. And, as the teacher builds a conjecturing atmosphere in the classroom, the students will learn from it, to develop their abilities to ask the questions themselves.

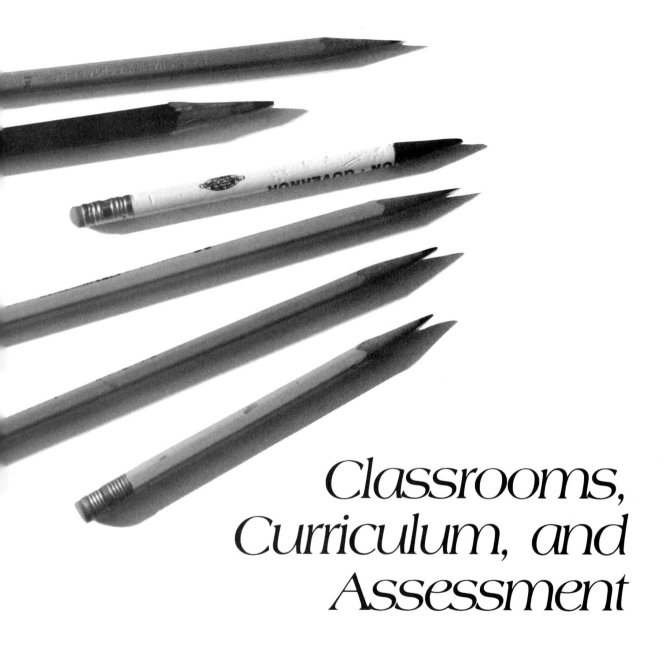

Chapter Six

Classrooms, Curriculum, and Assessment

Among the many questions that could be asked about teaching mathematics through natural learning processes, we find three to be crucial: How do I structure a classroom for such an approach? What does the curriculum look like? How do I assess the work and progress of students? We will address each of the three questions briefly in this chapter, in an effort to start a discussion that will, we hope, lead teachers to develop their own answers.

Classroom organization

There isn't one best method of classroom organization. A natural learning approach can be used with the whole class, with small groups, with learning centers, with contract systems, and with combinations of these. Teachers are probably best advised to continue with their current organization as they experiment with implementing natural learning conditions and processes. However, some principles may be helpful.

Group Work Is Not Necessarily Shared Work

One of the benefits of a natural learning approach is that students are encouraged to talk about their mathematics. Math is not a solitary activity but something to be discussed: with friends, with the teacher, in a conference with other students in the class, or with older or younger students. The talking is important for precisely the same reason it's important in language learning: Talking allows students to clarify their thinking, rehearse ideas, exchange ideas, get help, collect information, and reveal their thinking to the teacher.

We have found, therefore, that teachers adopt classroom organizations that reflect this need for discussion. Students rarely work on their own. In most cases, they have the support of a group. But group work does not necessarily mean shared work. In language classrooms, students work in groups, and they are given every opportunity to discuss their writing, but they essentially do their own work. In general, it is not shared writing.

We believe the same model should apply to mathematics. Students should work in groups and be encouraged to discuss what they are doing. But within the group each student should usually be working on his or her own math. On occasion, a shared activity may be appropriate. For example, students might work in pairs to make a plan of the school. However, if students are making something for measuring angles, they should each be expected to make his or her own angle measurers, to show aspects of his or her own thinking.

Whole-Class Activities

Some teachers ask the entire class to work on one activity, while others prefer to ask groups to attempt different challenges at the same time. Sometimes it is a question of resources. If it is easier to gather one set of resources, it might be best to engage the entire class in the same activity. However, limited amounts of equipment may make it impossible for all students to be engaged in the same activity at once, in which case smaller-group work makes more sense.

Whole-class activities serve several purposes. Sharing is best done in a large group, which is usually the whole class. Students learn by hearing what their colleagues have done. They collect ideas to try themselves or to extend or improve their own work. Sharing sessions provide an audience for mathematics and hence a reason for students to select their best mathematics for sharing. Both the selecting and the sharing helps develop an appreciation of quality.

The whole class can contribute to an activity over an extended period of time. Challenges such as finding interesting numbers or making numbers from 1 to 100 from the digits

1992 benefit when the entire class is involved. The teacher could place a sheet with the numbers 1 to 100 on a board with spaces for students to record their computations or explain why they find the numbers interesting.

We have referred in Chapter 3 to structuring the challenge. This is a process in which students use methods such as brainstorming to open up the possibilities inherent in a particular challenge and identify possible starting points. Structuring is often best done by the whole class together, so an extensive range of starting points will be available to all.

Groups Undertaking Different Activities

Many teachers like classrooms in which groups of students are engaged in different activities. If the assessment and planning processes described below are followed, teachers will need different activities for different students. In general, the same challenge will be suitable for a group of students, although possibly for quite different reasons. Because the challenges are open-ended, there is little risk that they will be entirely unsuitable for some students.

Because students individualize their responses to a particular challenge, one challenge is often enough to initiate a variety of classroom activities, as different groups of students follow their own lines of thinking.

Occasionally, a teacher may design a challenge for just one student, simply because that student needs to be challenged in a particular direction. Quite often, students will challenge themselves.

Learning Centers

Challenges lend themselves to use with learning centers. They are fairly discrete activities, the challenge itself can be presented with relatively few instructions, and some of the materials can be collected at the center. Because the challenges are open, they may be suitable for a large number of

This week's challenges.

students. Some teachers have found that the establishment of one or two learning centers can provide a low-risk introduction to the use of natural learning methods. As they and their students become familiar with challenges and with the approach in general, teachers can gradually extend math challenges until they compose almost the entire curriculum.

Learning centers can be established outside the classroom as well. Some schools have placed math challenge centers in the corridors and areas where parents congregate and have invited parents and students to try them out. Learning centers can also be temporarily transported to shopping centers or other community areas to allow community members to experience this style of math education for themselves.

If teachers do use learning centers, they need to ensure that the needs of individual students are met. Some students may find it difficult to get started on a challenge and need some initial help. Others may have particular needs that will not be met by a general challenge. Wherever possible, challenges should be designed around the needs of individual children or groups of children.

Challenge Libraries

Challenges can be used more than once. On each successive occasion, students will interact with it at a higher level, produce a more sophisticated response. So long as the challenge remains challenging, it can be used time and again.

Some teachers have found this feature of challenges to be quite an advantage and have therefore established libraries of challenges. Challenges are not discarded after they have been used in the classroom. Instead, they are pinned on a bulletin board or placed in a box or basket. Gradually, a library of challenges is built up. At certain times, students are allowed to look through the challenges for one that captures their attention and, with teacher approval, use it as the basis for their math work. (The idea could be extended to include unused challenges as well.)

Having a library of challenges available could be a means of assigning more responsibility to students, similar to open-choice reading. Of course, since teachers design many of the challenges and decide which ones will be retained in the library, they retain some control over curriculum coverage.

A used challenge box.

Calculators in the Classroom

We believe that calculators should be readily available to children of all ages almost all the time. Calculators are now so widely available in the community, and so regularly used in the workplace, that it is essential that students have a good working knowledge of them.

The availability of calculators in the classroom also allows young students to work on real math problems and learn about difficult concepts like subtraction of negative numbers. Students need no longer be limited to problems that involve only small numbers. If students can use calculators, they are better able to see the math involved in a particular problem, are no longer bogged down by the computations. Calculators can have a major impact on number work. The use of calculators by young students in the United Kingdom (Shuard 1990) has led to a more open number curriculum.

For young students challenges such as the following are enhanced by the use of calculators:

Write number sentences involving subtractions. Select the most interesting one for publication.

Write subtractions involving numbers from the 6 times table. What is the most useful thing you have found out?

Investigate the use of the minus key on the calculator. Record the different things you can make happen. Publish your most important findings.

Calculators are just as useful for allowing students to explore large numbers, place value, and square numbers. They are invaluable for learning about decimals and making change. Calculators can be very useful in allowing the exploration of number patterns and relationships with larger numbers. We have used the following challenge with teachers in workshops:

Exploring large numbers.

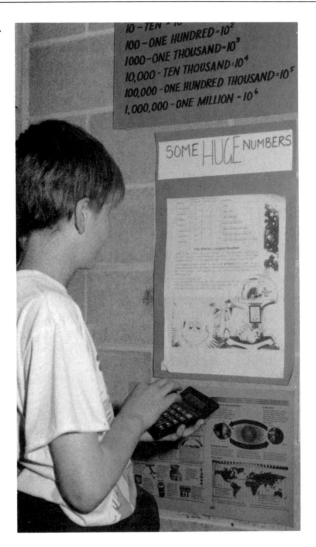

Write down the 37 times table. What patterns can you find? Select the most unusual for sharing.

Perhaps one of the best responses to this challenge came from four students working as a team in a math competition. Such events have traditionally involved closed questions that emphasize getting the right answers. Seeing no reason open-ended problems would not work as well, we organized a recent competition around challenges. Primary schools selected their most mathematically capable students, generally ten- to twelve-year-olds. The students worked in groups of four, and their work was assessed for accuracy, creativity, mathematical processes used, and presentation.

As part of their answer to the "37 times table" challenge, one team produced the following:

$$99 \times 37 = 3663$$
$$999 \times 37 = 36963$$
$$9999 \times 37 = 369963$$
$$99999 \times 37 = 3699963$$
$$999999 \times 37 = 36999963$$
$$9999999 \times 37 = 369999963$$
$$99999999 \times 37 = 3699999963$$

It always starts in 36 and ends in 63 and each time you times it with one more 9.

Parents

Natural learning processes are those that parents use when teaching young children their early language and mathematics. It's a case of doing what comes naturally. Hence a natural learning approach to school mathematics offers the exciting potential of deeply involving parents in supporting school mathematics, just as they support language learning by reading books with their children at night.

But parents are unlikely to support school mathematics if they feel they themselves cannot cope with it. They need to feel assured that they can handle the math and contribute to the learning. Conventional problem-solving approaches tend to alienate parents. The math looks very different and the risk of failure is great.

However, if math is presented as a series of open-ended challenges, there is virtually no chance of failure. The most useful challenges are so open-ended that parents and children can work together on the same challenge and achieve success at their own levels.

One school sent home a challenge with students from a first-grade class:

> Mark the 3 times table on the 1 to 100 grid (enclosed). What patterns can you find? After this, you might like to use an unusual times table. For example, try the 19 times table. Use a calculator to help. What patterns do you notice?

This is a very simple challenge, yet it provided the opportunity for both parent and child to work together on the same piece of mathematics.

It won't be easy to parallel for mathematics the support provided by parents who read to their children. Community attitudes are hard to overcome. But schools should quietly persist in sending suitable challenges home. And they should schedule regular parent meetings, during which teachers can explain the new approach and give parents a chance to try out a challenge in a nonthreatening environment. Of course, parents can best find out about the approach by visiting the classroom and seeing the learning that is taking place.

A new view of the mathematics curriculum—the big ideas

There is a dramatic change in our conception of the curriculum when natural learning conditions and processes are established in the classroom. The biggest change may be that teachers are no longer directly trying to teach a specific topic to particular students. Instead, teachers encourage students to clarify their thinking on a math theme and provide challenges to ensure that their thinking is extended and refined.

We would like the curriculum to be consistent with a natural learning approach to teaching and learning. Traditionally, the curriculum has been presented to teachers as a series of topics—and fragments of topics—to be covered. Some early childhood curricula have included, for students in consecutive years, such fragments as the following:

- Count to 10.
- Count to 20.
- Count to 100.

Such curricula have followed an adult logic that says that little people can only deal with little numbers. This is quite different from the reality revealed when students are allowed to decide for themselves which numbers to deal with. Children quickly realize that it is not much harder to count in hundreds than it is to count in ones, and very young children regularly included hundreds in their open number sentences.

Sometimes the curricula include very broad concepts such as "place value"—adult jargon for aspects of the number system that we hope students will come to use efficiently.

We would prefer to replace these concepts with the mathematical ideas they encompass. We wish to move away from a fragmentation of the curriculum and instead present mathematics holistically, just as parents naturally teach both language and math to their children. To do this, we have looked to the important ideas that we, as adults, believe that students should deal with during their schooling. They are the ideas that we expect students to use effectively as they become adults.

We have mentioned before the importance of adult expectations in language learning. It is the same for mathematics. As adults, we must hold up to students what we believe to be the important mathematical ideas, with a conviction that students will become effective users of these ideas.

We call these important ideas the "big ideas" of mathematics. They provide learners with a glimpse of the destination during the journey. They are the adult vision for mathematical learning.

The Mathematics Model Curriculum Guide for California (1987) refers to these basic ideas as "essential understandings:"

> They are the broad global ideas that expand or build, flower or evolve—that grow more complete and complex over time. . . . They are those worthy mathematical ideas that can be explored by the five-year-old as well as by the thirteen-year-old. (p. 15)

Just because big ideas are what adults hold out, they are not necessarily what students deal with directly. We have, therefore, broken each big idea down into its underpinnings, the ideas students will be working with more directly.

Here is a big idea: We extend our number system based on integers to include fractions, decimals, and percentages. We connect that idea with such underpinning ideas as:

- You can share things equally with the individual members of a group.
- The more people there are in a group, the smaller the equal share each person gets.
- Division can be expressed as a fraction.
- Every fraction has an infinite number of equivalent fractions.

101

*A new view of the
mathematics curriculum—
the big ideas*

Each of these underpinning ideas can then be linked to a number of challenges that teachers believe will help students develop their thinking about the idea. The idea that the members of a group can share things equally might be connected to this challenge:

What number of objects can you share equally
between three people? Four people? Etc. How can you
make sure each person gets the same?

This approach to the curriculum is currently being developed as a major curriculum project in Tasmania (Department of Education and the Arts, Tasmania 1992). Many groups of teachers are involved in deciding just what big ideas they would like students to deal with. They are then developing the underpinning ideas and the challenges associated with them and thereby providing support for classroom teachers. In this way, the curriculum is being constructed in the minds of some of the people who have to implement that curriculum.

Teachers have had to establish criteria for deciding which ideas they would like to include as big ideas. The consensus is that an aspect of mathematics qualifies as a big idea if:

- It is important for an understanding of an area of mathematics, or
- It is important for helping people act in the world.

That is, ideas are assessed according to their theoretical and practical importance.

Assessment

It should not be surprising, at this point, to hear that assessment in mathematics has much to learn from work in the assessment of language development. Gordon Wells (1986, p. 48) describes vividly what happens in language learning:

> All that is required is that [adults] be responsive to the cues that children provide as to what they are able to understand. Rather than adults teaching children, therefore, it is children who teach adults how to talk in such a way as to make it easy for them to learn.

If assessment is the technique by which teachers gather information to judge the progress of learners in order to help them learn, then Wells's description can fairly be called assessment. And what a contrast to our conventional thinking about assessment. The adult makes the assessment but it is the child who is in charge of the overall process. Children show adults where they are so that the adults can learn to respond in a way that will most help the further learning of the children. This is assessment in a natural learning context.

In language, there has been a movement away from formal testing and toward observational and descriptive methods of assessment. This has partly come from dissatisfaction with tests and the limited amount of information they can provide. It has also come from a dissatisfaction with reductionist approaches to assessment and with attempts to break language into the small components that can be easily tested. Such efforts may miss the major process, namely, meaning making. Language is a highly complex and holistic phenomenon for communicating meaning. Attempts to reduce a student's language learning to a small number of test scores are likely to be inadequate at best and can be highly misleading.

Teachers find they can use observational methods to learn much about children's concepts of language use, their strategies for processing language, and their attitudes. Armed with this information, teachers are then able to plan appropriate learning experiences.

Teachers of mathematics have traditionally been even more prone than language teachers to rely on tests. This is largely because mathematics teaching has traditionally been fragmented. Students have to master A before they can attempt to learn B. And testing programs are designed to check that the students has indeed learned A before they proceed further.

While the logic that A is easier than B may be clear to adults, difficulties arise when individual students have quite different learning sequences. B may well be more readily learned than A. However, if A is being tested, the test isn't measuring what the student knows, only what the teacher has been teaching.

The NCTM's *Curriculum and Evaluation Standards for School Mathematics* (1989) describes other difficulties with standardized tests.

> Furthermore, because of their format, standardized norm-referenced tests have difficulty measuring the generation of ideas, the formulation of problems, and the flexibility to deal with mathematical problems that are not well structured (i.e., problems similar to those encountered in everyday life). (pp. 201–202)

If students are going to deal with problems more like those people actually confront in the real word, and if students are to be assessed, it is necessary to abandon standardized tests (and, we would add, similar forms of formal testing) in favor of more appropriate assessment techniques.

A Holistic Approach to Assessment

In recommending a move toward natural learning processes, we are advocating corresponding changes in mathematics assessment. Challenges typically engage a vast array of the learner's knowledge, skills, and attitudes. These include prior knowledge; skills associated with interpreting the challenge and communicating the findings; analytical, computational, and pattern recognition skills; and values and attitudes toward mathematics and toward the learning environment in general. There are any number of acceptable responses to a challenge and a myriad of possible pathways to a solution.

Fortunately, challenges carry opportunities for a more appropriate form of assessment. They provide teachers with a window into the student's thinking, just as parents learn how best to respond to their children who are learning to talk. In open-ended situations, learners work at their own level and this, in itself, provides important information about student capabilities. Because risk taking is not punished and all answers are accepted as initial approximations, students are more likely to jump in and show just how they are thinking about a particular situation. This is in stark contrast to formal testing, in which students strive to duplicate the teacher's thinking as closely as possible.

What Is Assessment For?

Our position is that assessment is principally undertaken to assist learning. There are two ways in which assessment is most likely to assist learning. First, students can be helped to develop the ability to assess their own learning and, second, teachers can continually monitor the theories that students hold and, as a result, provide challenges designed to extend their thinking.

Assessment may also provide information to the learner, to the teacher, or to parents and the community. It may be used to determine accreditation, to evaluate teaching programs, or to rank students. But we believe that these are all subsidiary to its principal purpose. In designing any assessment program, educators must understand how the assessment will promote learning.

Student Self-Assessment

One of the conditions for natural learning is that learners accept responsibility for it. Teachers find that even young children are quite capable of deciding what they will learn and how they will learn it. Indeed, it is a natural process that teachers can support in the classroom. Wells (1986) has given us examples of infants who are in charge of the assessment processes and the improvement of their own learning.

One of the features of learning to speak is that many of the procedures are naturally self-correcting. If children do not manage to communicate by using a particular expression, they will try again, perhaps in a different way, adding gestures or pointing, until they get a response. The adult will usually model conventional usage, helping the child move toward it. Experimenting leads to success, rarely failure. Similarly, in schools, the conditions for learning mathematics should be arranged to include self-correcting mechanisms. For example, students should regularly communicate their knowledge about mathematical processes to others so that the parts that don't make sense can be identified and help provided.

The assessment process must reflect this atmosphere of responsibility if it is fully to support learning. Self-assessment is a powerful way to ensure that the responsibility for learning stays with the learner. Students need to be encouraged to monitor their own mathematics learning and reflect on it as part of refinement cycles. The first response to a challenge is unlikely to be the last. On many occasions, it is appropriate for students to try to improve their mathematics, with a particular purpose in mind. For example, the work may be prepared in order to be taken home, or to be published in the classroom, or to be communicated to students in another class. These goals require the students to assess the quality of their own work as they seek to improve it. We believe that this should be a routine part of classroom mathematics, with teachers ensuring that the reflective processes are in place but with the responsibility for the assessment remaining with the students.

Learners refine their theories as they learn. One set of theories we would like them to develop are theories about learning itself. This may not be quite so natural. Students need to be encouraged to reflect on their learning, on how they learned and why. If they are encouraged to do so, they can develop their reflective capacities and become independent learners.

It is important that teachers make it clear that students are engaging in assessment when they reflect on their work. It is also important that teachers help students to articulate their assessments. And it is especially important that such assessments be valued.

Observing Students to Plan Future Learning

Teachers have different responsibilities than learners have. Teachers are responsible for creating natural learning conditions in the classroom, for ensuring that students are challenged, for opening up areas of the curriculum, and for fostering learning processes. To do this, they must monitor, reflect on, and improve what happens in the classroom, and this requires making assessments of students' learning.

Again, we can draw metaphorically on Wells's observation that children teach their parents how to respond appropriately. Teachers must learn—from the students—about their students' developing ideas and then challenge the students to refine those ideas.

The type of assessment we prefer, because of its coherence with our approach to teaching and learning, is systematic, informal, continuous observation of students as they use mathematics in a variety of situations and for different purposes. Teachers collect a wealth of information as they observe students, far more than can be collected by any testing program. And this information is collected in context. It is not obtained in a formal situation disconnected from the learning. Teachers can respond immediately if required or take note for more leisurely reflection. And they collect information about student attitudes and feelings as well as about ideas and capabilities. It is a holistic process.

Teachers find it helpful to systematize the collection of this information. Otherwise, it is too easily lost in a busy classroom. Many of our teachers focus on a small number of students each day and try to observe their math and language work carefully. They may observe the students as they work in the classroom, they may sit in on an activity, or they may take the student (or group) aside for a conference on the progress being made with a particular challenge. Some teachers record a group working on a challenge and later analyze the tape.

The observations are often jotted down opposite a list of the students' names. Some teachers have expanded this into a grid that allows them to record the activity the student is working on, their observations about the student's work, and their ideas for possible future assignments and challenges. The documentation may look something like that shown in Table 6–1. These recordings link observations and planning. The teacher observes the student and decides what may be appropriate next.

Table 6–1. Recording observations.

Name	Challenge	Observation	Future work
Anne	Measure the ball	Used informal units again.	Make a cm measurer.
John R	Make a ruler	More interested in decorating his ruler.	Establish a purpose for using the ruler.

How Do I Know What Students Should Do Next?

Sometimes what a student should try next is obvious. A student who uses only one operation in working on number sentences needs to be challenged to try different operations. Someone who shows that she can operate with halves should be challenged to try using other fractions.

Sometimes, however, it is not obvious, particularly in areas in which the teachers themselves are less sure of the mathematics involved. Yet it is essential that students be challenged in all the areas of math that we, as adults, believe are important.

With the curriculum expressed as ideas (see the section on big ideas earlier in this chapter), the math can more easily be made part of the link between monitoring and planning. Teachers can document the ideas that a student is currently working with and then look for associated ideas that might be appropriate for future work. A teacher recorded the information in Table 6–2 after observing a student who had been challenged to find ways of dividing twenty objects into equal groups. Having seen the student readily divide a collection into four equal parts, the teacher decided that this student

A teacher collects observations of a student's mathematical thinking to be recorded in a planning book.

Table 6–2. Observations linked to ideas.

Idea worked on	Observation	Associated ideas	New activity
You can divide things into equal groups	She divided them into four equal groups	Single objects can be divided into parts	What is the most complicated shape you can divide into four equal parts?

needed to be challenged to divide single objects into fractions. Hence, the teacher chose to challenge the student to make complicated objects that could be divided into equal parts.

Assessment and planning can be effectively linked through the following process: Challenge, observe, and record the student's thinking; compare that with the mathematical ideas; reflect on your expectations for that student; then challenge the student again. While records of observations like those shown in Tables 6–1 and 6–2 are made primarily to assist learning, they are also valuable for other assessment purposes. In particular, they are helpful as a basis for discussing the progress of an individual student with his or her parents: They show parents, in simple language, what ideas their child has been developing and is currently dealing with.

The discussion of assessment concludes this book, and it strikes us that this rather sudden ending is appropriate. Like a good math challenge, our ideas cannot be set aside as long as there is interest in exploring them further. This is simply a beginning, a challenge in itself. We hope that teachers and other educators will accept the challenge: to explore and expand the possibilities for engaging students in a natural learning approach to math education, and to break down the barriers that prevent children and all learners from experiencing the pleasure of learning the lessons and language of mathematics.

At the beginning of Chapter 2, we describe the natural process of learning oral language—a fascinating, mysterious process. We end that discussion by stating that it is a stunning achievement. We close this book with the hope that teachers will open the necessary doors to enable their students to learn math as a natural process. We believe that in doing so they will find that they, and their students, will have taken part in another stunning achievement.

A great mathematician at work.

Bibliography

Baker, A., and J. Baker. 1990. *Mathematics in Process*. Portsmouth, New Hampshire: Heinemann.

———. 1991. *Maths in the Mind: A Process Approach to Mental Strategies*. Portsmouth, New Hampshire: Heinemann.

Baker, D., C. Semple, and T. Stead. 1990. *How Big Is the Moon? Whole Maths in Action*. Portsmouth, New Hampshire: Heinemann.

California State Department of Education. 1987. *Mathematics Model Curriculum Guide, Kindergarten Through Grade Eight*. Sacramento.

Cambourne, B. 1986. "Rediscovering Natural Literacy Learning: Old Wine in a New Bottle." Paper presented at the ESL Conference, Singapore.

———. 1988. *Natural Learning and the Acquisition of Literacy in the Classroom: The Whole Story*. Richmond Hill, Ontario: Scholastic-TAB.

Bibliography

Cobb, P., T. Wood, and E. Yackel. 1990. "Classrooms as Learning Environments for Teachers and Researchers." In *Constructivist Views on Teaching and Learning Mathematics*, edited by R. B. Davis, C. A. Maher, and N. Noddings. Reston, Virginia: NCTM.

Cockcroft, W. H. 1982. *Mathematics Counts*. London: Her Majesty's Stationary Office.

Department of Education and the Arts, Tasmania. 1992. *Mathematics K-8 Guidelines*. Hobart, Australia.

Dyson, A. H. 1982. "Reading, Writing, and Language: Young Children Solving the Written Language Puzzle." *Language Arts* 59(8):829–39.

Edmunds, J., and R. Stoessiger. 1987. *Investigating a Process Approach to Mathematics*. Hobart, Australia: Education Department of Tasmania.

———. 1990. "Using Natural Learning Processes in Mathematics." *Mathematics in School* 19(3):30–33.

Education Department of Tasmania. 1987. *The Pathways of Language Development*. Hobart, Australia.

———. 1988. *Competencies Through Science*. Hobart, Australia.

Felton, H., and S. Coman. 1986. *Links Between Related Arts and Basic Learning: A Trial Program at East Ravenswood Primary School*. Hobart, Australia: Education Department of Tasmania.

Fromewick, A. 1988. "The Resnick-Halpern Conjecture." *Arithmetic Teacher* 35(5):3.

Holdaway, D. 1979. *The Foundations of Literacy*. Portsmouth, New Hampshire: Heinemann.

Lakatos, I. 1976. *Proofs and Refutations: The Logic of Mathematical Discovery*. Cambridge: Cambridge University Press.

McIntosh, A. 1980. "Mental Mathematics—Some Suggestions." *Mathematics Teaching*, no. 91:14–15.

National Council of Teachers of Mathematics. 1989. *Curriculum and Evaluation Standards for School Mathematics*. Reston, Virginia.

Shuard, H., A. Walsh, and V. Worcester. 1991. *Calculators, Children and Mathematics*. London: Simon and Schuster.

Smith, F. 1975. *Reading*. Cambridge: Cambridge University Press.

Stoessiger, R. 1988. *Using Language Conditions in Mathematics*. Primary English Newsletter, no. 68. New South Wales, Australia: Primary English Teaching Association.

Stoessiger, R., and J. Edmunds. 1989a. "Metaphors for Mathematics." *Australian Journal of Reading*, no. 12:123.

———. 1989b. *Using Natural Learning Processes in Mathematics: A Report of the Improving Mathematics Project of National Significance*. Hobart, Australia: Education Department of Tasmania.

———. 1990. "The Role of Challenges." In *Language in Mathematics*, edited by J. Bickmore-Brand. Carlton, Australia: Australian Reading Association.

Stoessiger, R., and H. Felton. "Theory Refinement: A Practical Way of Linking Research to Practice and Policy Making." Paper presented to the annual conference of the Australian Association for Research in Education, Armidale, Australia.

Stoessiger, R., and M. Wilkinson. "Emergent Mathematics." *Education 3–13* 19(1):3–11.

Wells, G. 1986. *The Meaning Makers: Children Learning Language and Using Language to Learn*. Portsmouth, New Hampshire: Heinemann.

Whitin, D. J., H. Mills, and T. O'Keefe. 1990. *Living and Learning Mathematics: Stories and Strategies for Supporting Mathematical Literacy*. Portsmouth, New Hampshire: Heinemann.